A DIPLOMAT LOOKS AT AID TO LATIN AMERICA

Willard L. Beaulac

SOUTHERN ILLINOIS UNIVERSITY PRESS

Carbondale and Edwardsville

FEFFER & SIMONS, INC.

London and Amsterdam

COPYRIGHT © 1970, *by* Southern Illinois University Press
All rights reserved
Printed in the United States of America
Designed by Andor Braun
Standard Book Number 8093-0429-5
Library of Congress Catalog Card Number 70-95591

Contents

PROGRESS

Preface

I SHOULD LIKE to explain, first of all, what this book is *not*. It is not a technical treatise on development or development aid. It preaches neither balanced development nor unbalanced development. It contains no key to rapid economic and social progress—no "take-off point" that less developed countries can confidently expect to reach, no gimmick of any kind.

Hundreds of books and articles on development and development aid have been published since aid became a normal feature of international relations. Many of them are very useful and would be even more useful if aid-donors and aid-receivers were willing and able to take them seriously. Others contain a great deal of solemn nonsense, some of which may have served to retard development rather than hasten it.

What the present book offers is a view of aid to Latin America in the context of our diplomacy in that area. Aid is not carried out in Washington or in Cambridge or Berkeley, although it may have important effects in Washington. It is carried out in the more than sixty countries labeled undeveloped, or underdeveloped, or less developed, or developing, or modernizing, or whatever the "in" expression may be, that we are extending aid to. It is there that it has its principal effects and it is there that it can best be observed and appraised.

I have served as Ambassador to five Latin American countries as different from one another as Paraguay, which has no trouble qualifying as an underdeveloped country, and Argentina, which has a very doubtful claim to the title, and I have been responsible for the administration of aid in all of them. My comments reflect largely my own experience and my own observations and the experience and observations of colleagues with whom I have compared notes.

During my last two years in the Foreign Service I was Deputy Commandant for Foreign Affairs of the National War College in Washington. The National War College is at the apex of our system of military schools. The one-year course given to highly selected officers of our armed forces and the Foreign Service is intended to familiarize the students with the broad range of factors—political, economic, social, and military—that enter into the formulation of our national security policy. The War College class is divided into committees, and the committees are given problems to solve, some of them real and some hypothetical. Included are problems that our government has been facing for years without having found solutions to them.

However at the War College we succeeded in solving all these problems—on paper. In fact, we solved them so readily that there was a temptation on our part to wonder why people in the world outside the classroom who had the responsibility for handling the problems were not as intelligent or as perceptive as we were or did not have as much guts as we had. When we solved problems we didn't merely react. We acted. We always took the initiative, and we always won!

But then our students, all of them mature men with broad experience in the field we were studying, would recall that problems in real life are never solved that easily. In the classroom we always made people behave as we wanted them to. The United States Congress was always cooperative, and the political opposition always understanding. Foreign peoples always agreed with us as to where their true interests lay. General de Gaulle was on our team. The New York *Times*, and even the St. Louis *Post-Dispatch*, usually supported us, and when they did not people simply ignored them.

There is a great deal in this book about the Alliance for Progress and its progenitor, the Act of Bogotá. Those programs were based on the premise that if Latin Americans and Americans would only act as the planners wanted them to act, Latin America's problems would be solved and solved quickly. They were War College solutions of the problem of underdevelopment in Latin America.

When I was Ambassador to Paraguay the question arose in Washington as to whether our government should continue its wartime program of technical cooperation with Latin America after World War II had ended. It was an extremely important question—much more important than most of us realized at the time. It was concerned with nothing less than what kind of a world we would live in when peace had come, and whether a lasting peace might be possible. I was invited to present my views before a committee of the

Congress. I recommended that aid be continued. I have never altered that view.

Since that time the United States has invested some thirteen or fourteen billion dollars on economic and military aid to Latin America, but the results have not been what we and the Latin Americans had hoped for, and a skeptical United States Congress now seems inclined to scrap the programs or at least reduce them drastically. What I am suggesting here is that our programs not be scrapped but strengthened, not by spending more but possibly by spending less, in both money and manpower; not by doing more but possibly by doing less and doing it better.

The present volume stems from a series of lectures I delivered at Southern Illinois University. Some of the ideas I had expressed as early as 1961 and 1962 in lectures at the National War College and the Industrial College of the Armed Forces. During the years that followed I have tested the ideas and refined them through reading and discussion and by revisiting Latin America and observing our aid efforts on the spot. My ideas have not changed substantially since 1962, and I ascribe this to the fact that they are derived from the experience of many years of dealing with Americans and Latin Americans, in and out of government, and because they have to do principally with people, who change very slowly.

Carbondale, Illinois   *Willard L. Beaulac*
September 1, 1969

THE ACT OF BOGOTÁ

I. The Nixon Visit

MOST PERSONS would agree, I am sure, that in recent years the two phenomena of outstanding importance in our relations with the countries of Latin America have been the communization of Cuba and the Alliance for Progress. To these I would add an earlier phenomenon: Vice-President Richard M. Nixon's visit to South America in May of 1958. That visit was important in itself. It also was related to the other two phenomena, as they were related to each other.

Mr. Nixon's visit was highly publicized at the time and widely commented on then and later. The vice-president clearly considered the visit and the hostile attacks he was subjected to in several countries as helpful to him in his political career. "Just one month after my return from South America," he said in his book, *Six Crises*, "the Gallup Poll showed me leading Adlai Stevenson for the first time, and running neck-and-neck against John F. Kennedy. It was the high point of my political popularity up to that time."[1] The attacks on Mr. Nixon in South America undoubtedly were helpful to him. But they were far from being helpful to the United States.

Mr. Nixon's primary purpose in flying to South America, it will be recalled, was to be present at the inauguration of Argen-

---

1. Richard M. Nixon, *Six Crises*, (New York, 1962), p. 249.

tina's President Arturo Frondizi. Dr. Frondizi was the first person
to be elected president of Argentina after the fall of dictator Juan
Peron, and great importance was given to his election not only in
Argentina but in many other countries as well.

Of all the Latin American countries Argentina long seemed
the most likely to achieve greatness. Its people are of European
descent and highly literate. Its territory stretches from the sub-
tropics to the Antarctic. Its extensive pampa is one of the richest
food-producing areas to be found anywhere.

Argentina, then, has the basic requirements of greatness—
people, territory, and resources, but despite impressive early progress greatness has eluded her. Nevertheless, many Argentines,
and many non-Argentines as well, who have observed the country's failures with disbelief, have retained a degree of confidence
that one day Argentina will fulfill its promise. It seemed possible
that Frondizi's election, following the long period of Peronist
retrogression, might usher in that day.

President Eisenhower recognized the importance of Frondizi's election by naming Vice-President Nixon to head the Special Mission that was to attend his inauguration. In addition, and
for reasons that doubtless were closely related to the 1960 presidential elections in the United States, President Eisenhower
agreed that Mr. Nixon should take advantage of the opportunity
to make "good will" visits to other countries of South America.

I was Ambassador to Argentina at the time. Consonant with
its usual practice the State Department sent the embassy in Buenos
Aires detailed instructions concerning Mr. Nixon and his plans
and desires. The instructions contained such minutiae as Mr.
Nixon's taste in whiskey. For the record, the then vice-president
was partial to Jack Daniels which, of course, is very good and
very American. For the record, too, I had a supply of Jack Daniels
flown to Buenos Aires for the occasion. Mr. Nixon proved to be
very abstemious and most of the whiskey remained untouched.
Before he left, his staff loaded it aboard the vice-presidential plane
and carried it away, presumably back to its country of origin.

If Mr. Nixon had little interest in whiskey, he had other interests he attached importance to. One that gave the embassy
concern was his interest in meeting with students of the University of Buenos Aires during his stay in the city. We in the embassy were disturbed over this for several reasons. In the first place,

neither the university nor its students had expressed any wish to meet with Mr. Nixon, and a meeting seemed out of place in the circumstances of Mr. Nixon's visit. More important still, it was evident that in the real Argentine world a meeting between the vice-president of the United States and Argentine university students was almost bound to degenerate into a shouting match, a hostile confrontation between Mr. Nixon and Communist students that could bring no benefit to the University or to Argentina, or to relations between Argentina and the United States.

My own concern was so great that I flew to Washington and visited Mr. Nixon's office in the Capitol in an effort to dissuade the vice-president from his plan. I was unable to see Mr. Nixon but I did see Mr. Herbert Klein, his "chief of staff." I told Mr. Klein I hoped the vice-president would not persist in his plan. Mr. Klein told me he would pass on my observations to Mr. Nixon but he offered little hope that the vice-president could be dissuaded. "He has made up his mind," Mr. Klein said.

I also conveyed my apprehension to persons in the State Department but I had the impression that so far as the department and President Eisenhower were concerned Mr. Nixon would be left to do whatever he wished to do in Buenos Aires. That impression, it developed, was quite justified.

When it became clear that the vice-president was persisting in his plan to meet with Argentine students, embassy officials talked to the Rector of the University of Buenos Aires, Dr. Risieri Frondizi, who, it should be noted, is a brother of the then president-elect. Dr. Frondizi was dismayed when he heard of the vice-president's plan. He thought a meeting between Mr. Nixon and the students was inappropriate in the circumstances and that it could bring no good to anyone. He believed, rather, that only harm could result from it. Nevertheless in view of the vice-president's insistence Dr. Frondizi agreed to arrange a meeting with a small but representative group of students, provided it were a closed meeting and no advance publicity concerning it were given out.

Many distinguished foreigners besides the vice-president of the United States attended President Frondizi's inauguration. The presidents of several countries were there, and the ministers of foreign affairs of many others. Members of European royalty attended. Alexei Kosygin headed the delegation of the Soviet

Union. Each of these persons entered Buenos Aires quietly, as befits a guest at an inauguration or a wedding, and as Argentine official protocol contemplated. But a quiet entry did not enter into Mr. Nixon's plans.

One of Mr. Nixon's requests that the State Department had transmitted was that a convertible automobile be sent to the airport to carry the vice-president into Buenos Aires. The request, of course, was carried out. Mrs. Beaulac and I were waiting at the airport when Mr. and Mrs. Nixon flew in. Waiting to receive them in the name of the Argentine Government was the vice-president of Argentina, Admiral Isaac Rojas. He had ridden out in the government's newest and shiniest limousine and, after he had greeted the Nixons, he invited them to ride with him to the embassy residence where they would be living during their stay in Argentina's capital. Mr. Nixon declined this courteous invitation. Instead he invited Admiral Rojas to ride to town with him in his convertible. The admiral accepted, although he could not conceal a degree of surprise and discomforture.

Mr. Nixon then told me that he wanted to go through the business area of Buenos Aires on his way to the embassy. He wanted to make contact with the Argentine people, he explained. I passed Mr. Nixon's wish on to the police escort which was to lead the procession of cars into town.

A large plane filled with American newspapermen and cameramen had accompanied Mr. Nixon's plane to Buenos Aires. When the procession of cars finally departed from the airport, the convertible carrying the two vice-presidents was preceded by an open-bodied truck filled with cameramen, prepared and eager to record Mr. Nixon's every move.

At the edge of the city Mr. Nixon stopped the procession and sat himself on the rump of his car. He invited the Argentine Vice-President to do the same. There are few persons in the world more dignified and more conscious of their dignity than an Argentine admiral. Sitting on the rump of Mr. Nixon's convertible hardly fitted in with Admiral Rojas' concept of vice-presidential decorum. Nevertheless, he joined Mr. Nixon and even managed a smile when he did it.

The procession continued into the city. It was noon and the downtown streets were crowded with people going to and from lunch and enjoying the air and the sun. At one of Buenos Aires' busiest corners Mr. Nixon again ordered his car to stop. Without further warning he dismounted and plunged into the Argentine crowd, smiling broadly and offering his hand right and left to be shaken. The Argentines were delighted. They had never seen anything like this. They laughed and cheered. They shook hands with Mr. Nixon and patted him on the back while the television cameramen recorded it all for posterity and for the next day's 6:30 P.M. newscast in the United States. No camera was turned on Admiral Rojas who remained alone on the rump of the car, trying not to look critical or embarrassed.

From Mr. Nixon's viewpoint and from the viewpoint of television viewers in the United States and many other countries, his visit to Buenos Aires was a great success. Not even his meeting with the students struck a sour note, so far as the public was aware, but that, of course, was due to the careful planning of Risieri Frondizi.

As Dr. Frondizi had insisted, Mr. Nixon met with only a small group of faculty and students, not more than twenty in all, in an unannounced place at an unannounced time. No newspaper-men or cameramen were present. The meeting was what anyone familiar with Argentina might have predicted it would be. Communist students and students who leaned to communism took over the meeting which quickly degenerated into a series of insults directed at the United States and Mr. Nixon. No one's mind was changed. No one's opinions were modified. But at least the meeting was not televised. No harm was done to Mr. Nixon's public image or to the public image of the United States.

Meanwhile the vice-president was getting exactly the kind of publicity he wanted from the planeload of newspapermen and cameramen who followed him to most places he went in Buenos Aires, and who, of course, were much more interested in him than they were in President Frondizi. The publicity represented a gain for Mr. Nixon and for the United States, especially in countries other than Argentina. Argentines in general, after their first surprised gasp, took the vice-president's visit in their stride. They probably would have been just as cordial to Mr. Kosygin if the Russian had courted them as Mr. Nixon did.

But we in the embassy were disturbed. We asked ourselves what would have happened if Rector Frondizi had not planned the meeting with the students so carefully; if he had not limited it and restricted it and kept it out of the public eye. The publicity Mr. Nixon was receiving, contrived as most of it was, still was so favorable that we began to speculate concerning how long the international Communists would permit it to continue. That they had ways to put a stop to it none of us doubted. We did not have to wait long for an answer.

Vice-President Nixon flew from Buenos Aires to Asuncion, Paraguay, and then to La Paz, Bolivia. In both those capitals he had propaganda successes of reasonable dimensions. From La Paz he flew to Peru where disaster overtook him. Students and alleged students stoned him and spat at him in the streets of Lima and prevented him from visiting San Marcos University, where he had arranged to speak. He flew on to Caracas, Venezuela, where his life was placed in danger by extremists. President Eisenhower considered him in such peril in Caracas that he had American troops poised to land in Venezuela if the vice-president needed their protection, although how the troops could have got there in time to be helpful no one could explain.

What did the incidents involving Mr. Nixon prove? So far as the incidents in Caracas are concerned, they probably proved that Mr. Nixon should not have gone to Caracas at the time he did. No persuasive reason for his visit existed.

Venezuela was going through a trying period in her history. The dictator, Marcos Perez Jimenez, had just been overthrown and had taken refuge in the United States. Venezuelans were deeply divided on many issues; the meaning of democracy, the role of the military, the attitude toward foreign capital, especially American capital in the economically and politically important petroleum industry, and relations with the United States.

The new government had had little time to establish itself in power. It had only tenuous control in Caracas, the capital, even over its own followers. It was a splendid time for foreign officials looking for propaganda successes for their countries or themselves to stay away. A prudent and knowing United States government would not have permitted Mr. Nixon to go to Caracas when he did.

The Caracas incidents were serious in the sense that there was a real threat to Vice-President Nixon's life in Caracas, but the Lima incidents occurred first and had greater impact in the United States and other countries.

What did the Lima incidents prove? They proved, if they proved anything, that in Latin America extremists can bring about incidents of the kind that occurred almost anywhere they please, and almost any time they please. They proved little else. However, after our press had published millions of words about the incidents, after the commercial television had squeezed out every ounce of saleable sensation from them, and after the Administration and the political parties had made appropriate statements concerning them with one eye fixed on the 1960 elections, the United States, and the world in general, were left with the impression that a continent was hostile to us. Rarely has so much been blown up from so little.

Following the Nixon incidents our government went along with the concept of a hostile Latin America which had to be appeased through increased economic aid. What other explanation of the incidents could there be? The Administration couldn't very well take the view that what was basically involved, besides the rowdiness of a few people, was the imprudence of a youthful and ambitious vice-president. And Mr. Nixon's opponents, whatever their private views might have been, saw no political profit in adding domestic injury to foreign insult.

So it became axiomatic that it was not a handful of extremists and political punks who had demonstrated against Mr. Nixon in Lima; it was Latin America which was demonstrating against the United States in the person of Mr. Nixon. The enthusiastic receptions that Mr. Nixon had received in Argentina and Paraguay and Bolivia, and which had so excited the press and the television networks, no longer had any meaning, if indeed they were remembered.

A flood of statements and speeches came out of Washington. The general sense of these was that it was time to pay more attention to Latin America. Old charges that we were not doing enough for Latin America were revived and became official doctrine. The Lima and Caracas mobs were no longer seen as mobs. They had become soldiers in the revolution of rising expectations. The Voice of America stepped up its propaganda to Latin America, which overnight had become a prestige area for American diplomacy; an area in which the United States was in trouble, that is.

Latin Americans were at last getting the attention from

Washington they had long craved but had not received. It occurred to more than one of them that the Lima and Caracas mobs had supplied the key to greater consideration on the part of the government of the United States. These were not unfriendly persons. They were merely trying to be realistic.

Apologists for Mr. Nixon have said that it took something like the Lima and Caracas incidents to cause the United States to discover Latin America. There is no doubt that we discovered, or rediscovered, Latin America as a result of the incidents, but it was a Latin America that did not exist, although we have threatened to bring it into being—a sullen, hostile Latin America that has to be courted and appeased by gifts and flattery. The image of Latin America that was conveyed by our newspapers and our commercial television and that has been reflected in speeches of many of our highest officials, was an offense to the real Latin America. It certainly was not an image to base a policy on, but that is to a considerable degree what occurred.

2. The Cuban Revolution

IF THE NIXON INCIDENTS aroused concern over the attitude of Latin Americans toward the United States and what our government might do to improve it, the Cuban Revolution greatly increased that concern.

I was Ambassador to Cuba when the Revolution began. It did not begin in December, 1956, when Fidel Castro landed on the shore of Oriente Province from his refuge in Mexico and made his way with a handful of men to the Sierra Madre mountains. It did not begin earlier, in July of 1953, when Castro and another group attacked the Moncada barracks in Santiago. It began still earlier, on March 10, 1952, the day General Fulgencio Batista took over the Cuban government by force.

Three phenomena that are all too familiar in Latin America characterized pre-Castro Cuba. One was the sharp contrast between the affluent few and the many who were impoverished. A second was the widespread corruption in the Cuban government and the Cuban military forces. A third was the direct involvement of the military in the country's politics. Furthermore those phenomena existed in an exaggerated form. Cuba, in these respects, was almost a caricature of a Latin American country.

Cuba's wealthy were not merely wealthy but ostentatiously wealthy. Wealth existed to be flaunted. Cubans outdid each other in lavish expenditure and in conspicuous display. While a good servant who worked long hours was likely to earn no more than forty or fifty dollars a month, parties at the Havana Country Club had few rivals in terms of money spent on gowns, decorations, and imported liquors.

At the same time there was an important and growing middle class in Cuba. Labor legislation was "modern." In some ways it was overprotective, particularly of organized labor. Cuba already had one of the highest living standards in all Latin America, and it was continuing to rise. However, its economy was based on sugar, with its seasonal demand for labor, and no way to employ or properly sustain the thousands of sugar workers during the long "dead season" was ever found. Nor did other rural workers share adequately in Cuba's growing prosperity. Cuba's economy was rural-oriented but its politics were city-oriented.

Corruption in government is common in Latin America, although not as common as is frequently supposed. In many countries ethical standards are high, particularly in the light of the poverty which is pervasive in the area. But in Cuba corruption in government was so traditional that it was taken for granted, even admired in some cases. A Cuban politician who accepted graft was said "to bathe" (bañarse). It was reported admiringly of one leader well known in Cuban history that "he bathes but he also splashes." In other words he spread some of the graft around. Graft was perhaps the most common subject of political cartoonists, and Cubans perused the cartoons with glee. Laughing, of course, was better than crying.

Military intervention in politics is also, unfortunately, a common phenomenon in Latin America. But in many countries it is well intentioned or can be well intentioned. The military in Latin America have their quota of idealists, of earnestly patriotic men. Military intervention often fills a vacuum created by political irresponsibility or ineptness on the part of civilians. It sometimes is a substitute for anarchy. But the higher echelons of the Cuban military had no such worthy purposes. With notable exceptions military leaders were interested in two objectives—power and wealth, and they had their full share of both. If those phenomena existed in exaggerated form in Cuba, Fulgencio Batista's career illustrated them in a form that was exaggerated even according to Cuba's standards.

In 1933, when the revolution against the dictator, Gerardo Machado, began, Batista was a young army sergeant-stenographer. Cuba's army at the time was politicized but it was subordinate to the civilian government. It was probably too lethargic to be otherwise. It was led by officers some of whom rarely showed up at their places of command except to collect pay checks. In reality, it was run less by its officers than by its noncommissioned officers, by those who could be depended upon to be on the job. It was not so difficult as it might have seemed, therefore, for the sergeants, under dynamic young Fulgencio Batista, to take over control of the army. Nor was it too difficult for Batista, with his natural capacity for leadership, to become the power behind the throne in making and unmaking presidents and in dictating to them.

I served in Cuba twice, the first time from 1937 to 1941 as embassy counselor. Federico Laredo Bru was president of Cuba at the time, but the then Colonel Batista was running the government from his office in Camp Columbia. I was the embassy's principal contact with Colonel Batista and I came to know him well. Batista had scant formal education but he nevertheless was well read. His determination to learn never lapsed. He was an enthusiastic student of Abraham Lincoln and, ominously, also of Benito Mussolini. Able, hard-working, intelligent, and affable, he was a refreshing contrast to the stereotype of a Cuban military leader.

Batista became a candidate for the presidency in 1940 and won in free elections. He was a popular president and in Cuban terms an effective one. When his candidate to succeed him lost at the polls, Batista turned over the reins of government peaceably to the candidate who won, and left Cuba. Before taking up residence in Florida he made a tour of Latin America where he was acclaimed an apostle of democracy. In reality, however, Batista had lost the idealism that may have prompted him in his earlier political career. He had become wealthy. He had shared wealth and power with his colleagues in the armed forces, who remained the arbiters of political power after Batista's departure.

Batista's taste for wealth and power did not diminish after he left the presidency, and 1952 found him once more in Cuba and once more a candidate for the presidency. But the former president no longer had the appeal he once had for Cuban voters, and when he concluded he could not win the presidency at the polls, he took over the government by force with the support of the same military leaders who had shared power with him during his elected presidency.

The Cuban people were shocked and dismayed at Batista's action. They had become accustomed to corruption in government and tolerated it, or pretended to. Some doubtless hoped to share it. But free elections had become a tradition, or Cubans thought they had. With all their inadequacies Cubans thought they had achieved political maturity, at least in the electoral sense.

Governments might be corrupt and ineffective, but at least they could be replaced by orderly means. But Batista destroyed that illusion. They never forgave him.

The American embassy in Havana, in its despatches to Washington, could predict with confidence that Cubans, thinking and acting Cubans that is, would reject Batista; that it might take them a year or it might take them longer, but that they would reject him. And that is what they did.

If Batista and his associates had been corrupt during his first presidency, their corruption knew no bounds during the nearly seven years he served as president following the 1952 *coup*. Public resistance to the Batista regime, with its contempt for the constitution and its corruption, grew in intensity and violence. Repression by the government became more and more severe and more senseless and provoked still greater resistance. The Batista regime, rotten to the core, disintegrated in the face of token attack by organized groups. Batista was put to ignominious flight, more by the contempt of Cubans than by the limited military force that was used against him.

The Cuban Revolution was middle class and city based. It was supported by many who frequented the Havana Country Club—"oligarchs" in the lexicon of the Communists and, later, of the Alliance for Progress. The Communists joined it only on the eve of victory. Neither the peasants nor the dispossessed had much to do with it. Most of them, to the extent they thought in political terms, had long been admirers of President Batista.

The Cuban Revolution was a revolution to restore democracy to Cuba. It was a revolution to return Cuba to the constitutional path, to restore free elections and other political freedoms. Those aims were proclaimed by Castro and other revolutionary leaders. They were what Cubans fought for and what some died for. But the government of the United States, at least those persons in government whose opinions were decisive, interpreted the Cuban Revolution to be a "revolution of rising expectations" of the kind our global orators and some of our political scientists continued to warn us of, and they believed that somehow it was directed against the United States as well as against the government of Fulgencio Batista.

3. Indecision

THE NEW REGIME in Cuba had been in control of the country little more than a year when it became evident to our government that something should be done about Castro. What was happening in Cuba was an international scandal and a reproach to the inter-American system and to our leadership in that system. Castro had assassinated hundreds of supporters and alleged supporters of the Batista regime following so-called trials that more closely resembled Roman circuses, with the added quality that some of them could be viewed "live" on American television and taped to the other American republics.

The Cuban leader had seized American and other foreign properties without real thought of compensation. He had launched a campaign of vituperative public insult against the United States, its elected leaders, and its armed forces, and he had tried, covertly and openly as well, to subvert governments in other American republics. His designs and some of his acts were no less aggressive than those of the North Vietnamese in an area nine thousand miles from our shores. And like the distant Vietnamese, Castro and his followers sought and obtained the backing of the international Communists in whose ranks they had enlisted.

Both the Charter of the Organization of American States and the earlier Rio de Janeiro Treaty of 1946 provide, in effect, that an act of aggression against one American state will be considered an act of aggression against all the American states, giving rise to the right of individual and collective self-defense. That the Cuban threat was real and not a figment of anti-Communist imagination was later demonstrated by the missile crisis of 1962.

But the United States government did not want to act alone against Cuba or as one of a group that made up less than the two-thirds majority contemplated by the Rio treaty in the case of collective action. Even the two-thirds majority would not have obliged any state to use arms against Cuba without its consent, but it would have conferred a moral authority that a lesser vote could not. And the United States government felt it would need that moral authority if it were to use force against the Cuban government. However, it doubted that it could get a two-thirds vote from the Organization of American States, and possibly it was right. Certainly it could not expect to obtain such a vote unless it demonstrated resolute leadership. This it never did or tried to do.

There is a rule in politics that says, "When in doubt take a trip." On the subject of Cuba President Eisenhower was very much in doubt. He was still indecisive in January 1960 when he announced that he would visit several countries in South America and talk to their leaders.

I was still Ambassador to Argentina and I received President Eisenhower in Buenos Aires as I had received Vice-President Nixon two years earlier. As in the case of the Nixon visit, the State Department sent me a long instruction concerning the president's likes and desires. For the record, President Eisenhower at the time was partial to Regis Royal Scotch whiskey. For the record, too, I had a supply of Regis Royal flown down to Buenos Aires and, as in the case of the Nixon visit, the president's aides placed most of it aboard the presidential plane which carried it and the president's party far away from Buenos Aires.

But there were few other similarities between the Eisenhower and Nixon visits to South America. Whereas Mr. Nixon had encountered hostility in several countries, President Eisenhower encountered only cheering throngs. There was no hostility to him from any source. I accompanied the president in his car as he rode through the streets of Buenos Aires receiving and responding to the frenetic plaudits of the Argentines. The president was deeply moved. "This is great," he said, more to himself than to me, as staid Argentine matrons leaped inches off the ground and yelled, "Ike, Ike!" The Communists were identified by their banners, but these were not critical of the United States or of President Eisenhower. They were critical only of Argentina's President Frondizi whom the Communists systematically opposed.

For those who tend to be impressed by the actions of crowds, it was easy to reach the conclusion that Argentine Communists were friendly to President Eisenhower. The truth, of course, was that they were acting in the spirit of Camp David. Their apparent friendliness to President Eisenhower was as much a matter of international Communist discipline as their hostility to Vice-President Nixon had been. Whether President Eisenhower realized that, I am not sure. Neither he nor Secretary of State Christian Herter nor the president's brother, Milton Eisenhower, both of whom accompanied him, talked to me about that phenomenon or about any other phenomenon related to Argentina or Cuba or Latin America during the president's visit to Argentina. Nor did they discuss such matters with my Deputy Chief of Mission whom I had sent to Rio de Janeiro, under the State Department's instructions, to accompany the president's group to Buenos Aires and to brief them on what they might expect to find in Argentina. They never found an opportunity to talk to him.

The president did have a "summit meeting" with President Frondizi on a lonely island near the Argentine resort of Bariloche, in Patagonia. Although it is clear that the presidents discussed Cuba and of course economic development in Argentina, I never learned exactly what they said nor did the State Department. Neither the secretary of state nor the American ambassador attended the meeting. Only one American other than the president was there. He was the president's interpreter, a man who knew Spanish as well as English but had little understanding of the subjects the two presidents discussed. Nor is there any reason to believe President Eisenhower had the background to understand much of what President Frondizi was saying to him, which had to do mostly with things that concerned President Frondizi and Argentina.

For weeks after President Eisenhower left Argentina, President Frondizi would say to me, "President Eisenhower said" this, or "President Eisenhower said" that. I knew in most cases that President Eisenhower had not meant to say what President Frondizi had quoted him as saying, but I knew also that President Frondizi thought that President Eisenhower had said those things —a melancholy commentary on the utility of summit meetings. President Eisenhower and his party also visited other Latin American countries where other summit meetings were held, again with knowledgeable officials excluded. In all his meetings with the South American presidents, President Eisenhower discussed

Cuba. More probably he listened to what the other presidents had to say about Cuba.

Following his return to Washington, President Eisenhower was visited by a number of high-ranking officials of Latin American countries who talked to him and to members of his cabinet about Castro and Castroism. He, of course, continued to give a great deal of thought to Cuba and to what Latin American political leaders had said to him. But he remained indecisive.

Before I left Argentina in the summer of 1960, I was instructed to call on President Frondizi and convey to him our suggestion that a meeting of foreign ministers of the American republics should be called to consider the problem that Castro had created for the hemisphere. Knowing that Frondizi, an astute and experienced political leader, would want to know what plan we would be likely to present at such a meeting, I called the Department of State before approaching him and asked what our plan was. The department replied, in effect, that we had no plan, that we were going to play this one by ear.

I called on President Frondizi and conveyed our government's suggestion. "What plan will your government present at the meeting?" he asked. I replied that we would not present a plan, that we would play it by ear. The president stared at me in disbelief.

Meanwhile the Soviet Union's role in Cuba had become bolder. Chairman Khrushchev himself blustered, although it was later clarified that he was speaking in a "figurative" sense, that in case of necessity Soviet artillerymen could support the Cuban people with rocket fire. The spirit of Camp David had vanished.

President Eisenhower took public cognizance of Khrushchev's threat. On July 9, 1960, he said, "I affirm in the most emphatic terms that the United States will not be deterred from its responsibilities by the threats Mr. Khrushchev is making." And he added, significantly, "Nor will the United States, in conformity with its treaty obligations, permit the establishment of a regime dominated by international communism in the Western Hemisphere."

Five days after President Eisenhower's riposte to Mr. Khrushchev the State Department declared that "the principles of the Monroe Doctrine are as valid today as they were in 1823 when the Doctrine was proclaimed" and that the United States government "consequently reaffirms with vigor the principles expressed by President Monroe."

Latin Americans as well as Americans heard those statements and many Latin Americans accepted them. The statements, if they meant anything at all, meant that the United States would rid the continent of Castro and the Communist presence in Cuba, alone if necessary. We had ample reasons for wanting to do that, we had the power to do it, and we had the responsibility that accompanies power. But in retrospect the statements meant little or nothing.

As time went on and Castro grew more confident and aggressive, thinking persons in Latin America became worried. It appeared to many that Castro's daring, his ruthlessness and his studied insolence had paralyzed the United States into inaction, as they doubtless were intended to. Through our embassies we kept the Latin American governments informed in great detail of the sins of the Cuban regime and of our fear that Castroism would spread beyond Cuba. Through stepped-up USIA broadcasts we also kept the Latin American man on the street informed of our fears, or tried to. The American news agencies and the American press joined in this exercise with enthusiasm. Our government and the press fed from each other's alarm and conveyed a measure of that alarm to Latin America and, unfortunately, also to persons who might be contemplating investment in Latin America. Yet we evidently had no plan for altering the course of events except to train some Cuban exiles, whom a later administration would dump ignominiously on the shore of the Bay of Pigs to be killed or captured by Castro's militiamen, and to consult with our Latin American friends who we must have hoped would be more resourceful than we in meeting the Castro problem.

4. Act of Bogotá

ON JULY 11, 1960, President Eisenhower held a news conference at the summer White House in Newport, R.I. So far as I know, the statement he made came as a surprise to our country's diplomatic representatives in Latin America. It also came as a surprise to some officials of the State Department who were intimately concerned with Latin American affairs.

The president revealed in the first paragraph of his statement the degree to which he had been influenced by his own conversations with Latin Americans. He said,

> During my trip to South America in February and in numerous talks in Washington, I have obtained the views of leading Latin American statesmen on the problems which their countries and the area in general now face. They have told me of the aspirations and needs of their peoples for homes and land and a better life, and of their efforts to meet those needs.

President Eisenhower then referred to a forthcoming meeting of ministers of foreign affairs of the American republics which was to consider "matters of supreme gravity in the Caribbean area; matters that invoke a challenge to the ideals and purposes of the American community." The principal matter of supreme gravity clearly was the Castro matter, although President Eisenhower did not mention it specifically in his statement.

The president went on to speak also of a meeting of economic representatives of the American republics to be held in Bogotá, Colombia, in September. He explicitly linked the two meetings. "I believe it would be well for me to state the basic ideas which will guide the United States participation in these forthcoming meetings," he said. The ideas he stated were:

> *First,* widespread social progress and economic growth benefitting all the people and achieved within a framework of free institutions are the imperatives of our time.

Second, our nation's history and traditions place us in accord with those who seek to fulfill the promise of the future through methods consistent with the dignity of free men. Our interests and sympathies are with them.

Third, a new affirmation of purpose is called for in our cooperation with friendly developing countries in their efforts to progress.

The president then proceeded to list the "specific needs" he felt "must be met through cooperative action."

First, We need to consider with the other American Republics practicable ways in which developing countries can make faster progress in meeting their own needs and ways in which their friends can most effectively cooperate with them. A better knowledge and mobilization of resources, their more effective use, and the improvement of legal and institutional means for promoting economic growth are among the subjects which require special consideration.

I have in mind the opening of new areas of arable land for settlement and productive use. I have in mind better land utilization, within a system which provides opportunities for free, self-reliant men to own land, without violating the rights of others. I have in mind housing with emphasis, where appropriate, on individual ownership of small homes. And I have in mind other essential minimums for decent living in both urban and rural environments.

Second, In our common efforts towards these goals more attention needs to be given, in a manner which respects the dignity and rights of all, to improving the opportunities of the bulk of the population to share in and contribute to an expanding national product. Soundly based economic and social progress in any of our countries is of benefit to all. Each nation must of course resolve its own social problems in its own way and without the imposition of alien dogmas.

Third, Within this framework we need to consider whether there are better ways to accelerate the trend which is already evident toward greater respect for human rights and democratic government based on the will of the people as expressed in free and periodic elections. The United States with its tradition of democracy is opposed to tyranny in any form—whether of the left or of the right.

Leaving no reason for doubt concerning United States leadership in this newest effort to achieve rapid development in Latin America, the president added, "I have requested the Secretary of State to take the lead in conferring with our Latin American friends on these principles and purposes. Assuming their agreement, he will prepare for my approval as promptly as possible specific recommendations along these lines."

The meeting of ministers of foreign affairs that the president referred to was held at San José, Costa Rica, in August. Those attending were so far from being willing to recommend strong action against Cuba that the name, Cuba, does not appear in the documents approved at the meeting.

Latin American leaders gave no indication that they had altered the view that many of them had already expressed to President Eisenhower. That view, in essence, was that the most urgent problem facing their countries was not Cuba, or Castro (whom in any case they had faith we could handle, since we had indicated we would if necessary), but Castroism, which threatened to spread to the other American republics as we ourselves had publicly warned. The way to handle that problem, they reasoned, was for the United States to increase its aid to those republics as President Eisenhower had suggested in his public statement of July 11. At least enough of the leaders took that view to make it compelling.

The view had great advantages to Latin American leaders, especially to those whose countries were not directly threatened by Castro. Whereas strong action by the American republics against Castro might provoke reprisals from extremist groups in their countries, increased aid from the United States could be only a boon, not only economically but in terms of the political fortunes of the leaders. Or so they thought.

The thesis of course also had merit from President Eisenhower's viewpoint. He still was not sure in his own mind what should be done about Castro except possibly trying to isolate him politically and economically from the free world (which meant of course impelling him to even closer cooperation with the Communist world), but the president had in mind that stronger collective action against Castro might become necessary. However, he was not certain that the Latin American masses would support their governments in strong action so long as those masses were suffering the ills and privations that Castro claimed to be overcoming in Cuba. In the circumstances an enlarged aid program offered promise. It was something concrete. It was something the United States had experience with and could take credit for. It appealed to American idealism. And it could be made to work with money.

The economic meeting that President Eisenhower had referred to during his Newport press conference was held in Bogotá from September 3 to September 16, 1960. Technically it was a meeting of the Organization of American States' Special Committee to Study the Formulation of New Measures for Economic Cooperation. Only a few days before the committee met, the United States Congress, at the request of President Eisenhower, had authorized the appropriation of $500 million to establish a special inter-American social development fund to be administered by the Inter-American Development Bank. The fund would enable the United States government to extend "soft" loans for social development in Latin America.

Armed with this formidable offering, the United States delegation at Bogotá proposed a broad program of economic and social development in Latin America along the lines of President Eisenhower's Newport statement. All the Latin American republics except Castro's Cuba, which refused to sign, and Trujillo's Dominican Republic, which was not represented, approved the substance of the program and it became the policy of nineteen hemisphere governments.

The Act of Bogotá, in its preamble, notes that

the preservation and strengthening of free and democratic institutions in the American Republics requires the acceleration of social and economic progress in Latin America adequate to meet the legitimate aspirations of the peoples of the Americas for a better life and to provide them the fullest opportunity to improve their status.

"Preservation and strengthening of free and democratic institutions" was of course a euphemism for prevention of Castroism.

Under the heading, "Inter-American Program for Social Development," the Act of Bogotá recommended:

Measures to improve rural living and land use,
Better laws on land tenure,
Improved agricultural facilities,
Review of tax systems and fiscal policies,
Land reclamation and resettlement projects,
Construction of farm-to-market roads,
Improved housing and community facilities,
Expansion of homebuilding industries.

These of course were all excellent purposes which Latin Americans had long had in mind but which had proved to be extremely difficult to attain with the human and material resources they had available to them.

The distinctive feature of the Act of Bogotá, later to be incorporated into the Alliance for Progress, was that social improvement was given clear priority over economic improvement. Certain Latin Americans had long urged that the United States help to finance a social improvement program. The new element was the United States government's willingness to give priority to social improvement and to support it with a special half-billion dollar contribution. It was this support that chiefly moved the Latin American governments to accept the program and that permitted the United States government to take substantial credit for it.

One State Department spokesman later recalled, "We came to the conclusion—and submitted to the delegates at Bogotá—that the hemisphere's social problems demanded at least as high priority as its economic [problems]." He went on to say, "Latin Americans, even those who agreed with us and our thesis at Bogotá [there plainly were some who did not] are appalled at the enormity of the task ahead." Then, with remarkable prescience, or recognizing remarkable prescience on the part of the Latin Americans, the State Department representative continued

They [the Latin Americans] wonder—from their past observation of our reactions—whether we may not soon tire of the task, lose heart, because it does not progress steadily and uniformly, does not follow directions we consider to be the right directions. In short, they ask themselves whether sooner or later the United States will not abandon Latin America to its fate. Our task, therefore, is not only to provide aid and technicians but leadership with great understanding.

The Latin Americans were wondering, in other words, whether we might not be starting something we could not or would not help to finish.

One feature of the Act of Bogotá that gave concern to some members of the American delegation as well as to American and Latin American observers was the slight attention given to private capital, which had been an essential ingredient of economic and social progress in Latin America in the past and doubtless would have to be in the future.

The role private capital would be permitted to play would depend directly on the treatment it might receive from Latin

American governments. That treatment, in the year 1960, left much to be desired in many countries, but the representatives of the American republics at Bogotá skirted the problem. Representatives of many of the Latin American governments had no stomach for strengthening the role of private capital, particularly foreign private capital, and the United States representatives were more interested in dimming Castroism's prospects in Latin America. Social improvement today rather than economic and social improvement tomorrow seemed to them to offer the best hope of containing Castroism.

The Act of Bogotá was principally a list of intentions. Those intentions were reiterated and broadened in the Alliance for Progress, which President John F. Kennedy launched a few months later.

ALLIANCE FOR PROGRESS

5. An Alliance Is Conceived

PRESIDENT KENNEDY, IN HIS inaugural address, said,

To those people in the tents and villages of half the globe struggling to break the bonds of mass misery, we pledge our best efforts to help them help themselves, for whatever period is required—not because the Communists may be doing it, not because we seek their votes, but because it is right.

It is useful for presidents, in their public statements, to appeal to the higher instincts and purposes of our citizens, not only because the world is listening, but because the American people respond favorably to appeals to altruism and generosity. The Alliance for Progress is solidly based on both those virtues. But it has other bases too.

There was considerable truth in President Kennedy's statement that we do not give aid because the Communists may be doing it. Nevertheless, if the Communists were not giving aid and were not prepared to give it, and if they were not using aid and every other available device to turn governments and people against the United States, our aid problem would be simplified and greatly reduced. Communism, and the threat of communism, have been a constant spur to our aid efforts in Latin America as well as in other areas of the world, and our government has not hesitated to use the Communist threat as justification of our aid program when that kind of justification promised to be useful.

The Alliance for Progress, like its progenitor the Act of Bogotá, was a device for combating Castro and Castroism. Castro's claim that he was making it possible for the underprivileged in Cuba to improve their living standard, and that he was determined to do the same in other Latin American countries, impelled us to embark on a program that we made certain was different, and would sound different, from the aid programs we had been carrying out for years in Latin America. And in launching the Alliance for Progress and, before that, the Act of Bogotá, our government was, in a real sense, seeking the votes of Latin Americans. It was seeking their votes against Castroism and in favor of possible strong action against the Castro regime in Cuba.

As a candidate for the presidency, John F. Kennedy had taken an extreme anti-Castro position. During a campaign speech on October 25, 1960, he had said of the Republican candidate,

Mr. Nixon hasn't mentioned Cuba very prominently in this campaign. He talks about standing firm in Berlin, standing firm in the Far East, standing up to Khrushchev. But he never mentions standing firm in Cuba. And if you can't stand up to Castro, how can you be expected to stand up to Khrushchev? The transformation of Cuba into a Communist base of operations a few minutes from our coast— by jet plane, missile or submarine—is an incredibly dangerous development to have been permitted by our Republican policy-makers.

It is unlikely that Mr. Kennedy fully realized at the time how "incredibly dangerous" the Cuban development was. Despite his taunting of candidate Nixon, Mr. Kennedy as president never stood up to Castro. Nevertheless, the Cuban missile crisis more than justified his fears concerning a soft policy toward Castro, and ironically it was President Kennedy himself who was compelled to stand up against Cuban-based Soviet aggression aimed at the United States and the other American republics.

The United States government took great credit for determination and decisiveness in compelling Russia to remove its offensive missiles from Cuba in October 1962. But the alternative to decisive action was to submit to Russian nuclear blackmail in a geographical area that is vital to our security and where we have overwhelming military strength.

The Latin American countries have been praised for supporting the United States in its quarantine of Cuba. Our government has been particularly fulsome in praise of its Latin American allies. But it is equally difficult to see that those countries had much choice in the matter. The Russian threat was evident and grave. The Latin American countries depend for their survival upon United States military strength and United States readiness to use that strength if necessary. And they are committed, by formal treaty, to cooperate in meeting threats to their security and to ours.

Besides, the United States had announced its decision to quarantine Cuba *before* it asked for Latin American support. Refusal to lend support would not have deterred the United States from acting. It would, however, have revealed the Latin American countries as unwilling to give even token support to our effort to protect them, as well as ourselves, against a real and imminent danger, the kind of danger that they are committed by treaty to help repel. The quarantine of Cuba succeeded in compelling the Russians to withdraw their missiles from the island. Where success was lacking was in permitting the missile problem ever to arise in the first place. The United States and the countries of Latin America share responsibility for that lack of success.

While President Kennedy obviously did not anticipate the missile crisis, Cuba was very much on his mind from the beginning of his administration. The Bay of Pigs episode, the "perfect failure" as it has been called, was a traumatic experience for him. Nevertheless, his language remained as aggressive, and perhaps as devoid of meaning, as President Eisenhower's had been during an earlier period. Speaking to the American Society of Newspaper Editors on April 20, 1961, he said,

But let the record show that our restraint is not inexhaustible. Should it ever appear that the inter-American doctrine of non interference merely conceals or excuses a policy of nonaction—if the nations of this hemisphere should fail to meet their commitments against outside Communist penetration—then I want it clearly understood that this Government will not hesitate in meeting its primary obligations, which are to the security of our nation.

Should that time ever come [he continued], we do not intend to be lectured on "intervention" by those whose character was stamped for all time on the bloody streets of Budapest. Nor would we expect or accept the same outcome which this small band of gallant Cuban refugees must have known that they were chancing, determined as they were against heavy odds, to pursue their courageous attempt to regain their island's freedom.

Speaking of the rebel commander at the Bay of Pigs, the president said, "He has gone now to join in the mountains countless other guerrilla fighters, who are equally determined that the dedication of those who gave their lives shall not be forgotten and that Cuba must not be abandoned to the Communists. And we do not intend to abandon it either." The president's verbal offensive against Castro and Castro Cuba was just as positive and just as forceful as his verbal offensive against Castroism in the other American republics had been when he launched the Alliance for Progress only three weeks earlier.

Candidate Kennedy was familiar with the Eisenhower administration's economic program for Latin America before it was presented at Bogotá, and he planned, if elected, to carry it out, but with more verve and flair. A group of Kennedy advisers drawn from political, university, and business life, met at the Faculty Club of Harvard University and on December 19, 1960, subscribed to a paper entitled, "Alliance for Progress—A Program of Inter-American Partnership." The paper set forth most of the principles that eventually were embodied in President Kennedy's own Alliance for Progress. Many of these, of course, already were contained in the Act of Bogotá. The signers made clear that the proposed Alliance was directed squarely at Communism and Castroism in Latin America.

The Sino-Soviet alliance [they said] is actively working to topple these democratic leaders [in Latin America] in the conviction that many nations of Latin America are ripe for a take-over. We believe that unless the United States adopts new postures, this Sino-Soviet goal is attainable.

In these circumstances [they continued] United States policy must be based on the recognition that Mr. Castro is not a cause but a symptom.

Preoccupation with the "image" of the United States in Latin America was foremost in the signers' minds. They said,

There exists at present in the minds of many Latin Americans an image of the United States as interested in monetary and military advantage far more than in human welfare. The United States is viewed as sympathetic to reactionary, undemocratic and repressive governments and leaders in Latin America. In the absence of tangible support for new effective programs, that image will sharpen. If it does, and if the frustrations of Latin Americans are not relieved, they will turn increasingly to extremist political leaders who will ally themselves with the Communist powers, thus adding to the already dangerous momentum of the Sino-Soviet drive to engulf the Americas.

The Harvard Faculty Club planners were applying the "lessons" of Lima and Caracas to United States policy toward Latin America. Also in the planners' minds was the "one-minute-to-midnight" syndrome. "The election of Senator Kennedy has excited expectations and hopes throughout Latin America," they said. "This creates a fresh opportunity and challenge for the United States and for democratic leaders in Latin America . . . This opportunity may be the last," they noted dismally.

That the United States was largely to blame for Latin America's failure to progress was implicit in the document. Numerous ways in which the United States might improve its attitude were noted. "The United States will likewise have to abandon outmoded policies, such as restrictions against lending to government-owned mineral and other enterprises," the signers warned. Translated into real life this probably meant, among other things, that the United States government should undertake to finance the Argentine government's petroleum monopoly, which has been the origin of so many of Argentina's economic and political woes, and official monopolies in other Latin American countries.

The signers of the document indicted not only United States policy toward Latin America but also those who had carried it out. They recommended that United States diplomatic and consular representation in Latin America be upgraded "drastically" and that the accent should be on youth. "Professionally competent young men, with a sympathetic understanding of the revolutionary ferment in Latin America, are needed in our overseas posts," they noted.

The document referred to the

legitimate demands of long overdue reforms which have been either ineptly met or ignored by many regimes in Latin America and have failed to evoke adequate support from United States policy makers.

While economic growth is essential to the creation of tolerable conditions of living [the document continued], social reform is no less essential in giving the broad majority of the people a greater participation in the benefits of growth. This is the meaning of the social infrastructure: The investment in people through education, health, housing and land of their own. The emphasis given these objectives in the Act of Bogotá must be sustained.

It further noted that "development of self-sustaining economies is the target." "In many Latin American countries this is feasible within a decade," it noted optimistically. The need for public investment was stressed. "Public investment supported by loans from U.S. Government and international agencies, such as the IDB and the IBRD, must play a major role—perhaps the predominant role in the immediate future." And it went on to suggest that "there is need also for substantial capital on a 'soft-loan' basis—that is, very long-term loans at low rates of interest—and for grant funds."

The document's signers were intent on the United States taking the initiative in launching the Alliance. "It is indispensable that the initiative come from the United States," they said. "The initiative should be undertaken in a manner that will produce an impact comparable to General Marshall's historic offer [to Europe]."

President Kennedy did his best to carry out that advice. Addressing a meeting of Latin American ambassadors called to the White House to hear him, the president said on March 31, 1961.

I have called on all the people of the hemisphere to join in a new Alliance for Progress—Alianza para el Progreso—a vast cooperative effort, unparalleled in magnitude and nobility of purpose, to satisfy the basic needs of the American people for homes, work and land, health and schools—techo, trabajo y tierra, salud y escuela.

Secondly, I will shortly request a ministerial meeting of the Inter-American Economic and Social Council, a meeting at which we can begin the massive planning effort which will be at the heart of the Alliance for Progress.

President Kennedy patently was not consulting the Latin American ambassadors concerning what should be done to advance the interests of their countries. Like President Eisenhower before him, he was making an announcement to them.

6. Alliance for Progress

WHAT IS THE Alliance for Progress?

Speaking to the members of the United States delegation to the Punta del Este Conference, at which the Alliance was born, President Kennedy said, "Alliance for Progress was a phrase in January." A phrase of the president's, he meant. "It became a proposal in March," he continued. The proposal, too, was President Kennedy's. "Now it is a fact," he concluded. But he did not explain what the fact was, and it is not easy to explain it today.

The Alliance for Progress is not an alliance in any formal sense. The commitments it embodies are not on the same high level as, for example, the treaty commitment of the American republics to cooperate in resisting aggression or their commitment not to intervene in one another's affairs. President Kennedy and others referred to the Alliance as a "partnership," a word that the planners at the Harvard Faculty Club had used. José Figueres, former president of Costa Rica, and an early supporter of the Alliance, referred to it in a moment of enthusiasm as nothing less than "the third entry of the United States into an embattled world." The first two entries, he explained, were into the First and Second World Wars. Subsequently, Secretary of the Treasury C. Douglas Dillon felt constrained to warn the other American republics that the Alliance was not merely a loan program. He must have felt that many of them thought it was.

The Alliance has been a special subject of oratory in the United States. Secretary Rusk has said,

For us, the Alliance is a special part of an indivisible whole. For it rests on those indissoluble ties of common culture and common interest, which have always bound our nations together. It rests on the realization that this Hemisphere is part of that western civilization which we are struggling to protect and that many of the highest values of that civilization have found their richest expression in the life of the nations to our south. It rests on the special responsibilities of the United States in this hemisphere—responsibilities which exist independently of the Cold War, or a Soviet military threat, or the demands of nations newly freed from colonial rule. It is an alliance which my country has joined because of our realization that the destiny of the United States is irrevocably joined to the destiny of our sister republics of the New World.

Those who know Secretary Rusk will agree that he meant every word he said. And, of course, he might have gone even further in his support of the Alliance. The United States not only joined the Alliance, as the secretary modestly pointed out, it conceived it as we have seen.

If it is difficult to explain to ourselves and to others precisely what the Alliance is, its objectives are clear. They are:

1. Insure that no country will have an economic growth rate of less than 2.5 percent.

2. Increase income and living standards of the needy while at the same time a higher proportion of the national product is devoted to investment.

3. Achieve economic diversification.

4. Raise greatly the level of agricultural productivity; reform tax laws, demanding more from those who have most; redistribute the national income.

5. Encourage agrarian reform.

6. Eliminate adult illiteracy and assure that by 1970 every child in Latin America will have access to six years of primary education.

7. Increase life expectancy at birth by a minimum of five years.

8. Increase the construction of low-cost houses for low-income families and provide necessary public services to both urban and rural centers of population.

9. Maintain stable price levels, avoiding inflation or deflation.

10. Strengthen existing agreements on economic integration.

11. Prevent the harmful effects of excessive fluctuations in the foreign exchange earnings derived from the export of primary products.

In short, the Alliance was aimed at accomplishing basic objectives in the economic and social field that the framers considered desirable and that the other American republics had been unable to accomplish during their long history. And, reflecting the view of the planners at the Harvard Faculty Club, the signatories of the Alliance were "pledged," in the words of one State Department official, to accomplish those objectives in the course of one decade.

What new instruments does the Alliance offer for accomplishing what it has not been possible to accomplish in the past? The chief instrument is a heightened resolve of the Latin American peoples to improve their own contribution to the process. That resolve is expressed in the Charter of Punta del Este, which outlines the Alliance. It has yet to be demonstrated sufficiently in practice.

A corollary instrument is the resolve of the United States government to increase and continue its contribution to the process.

To supplement the domestic efforts of such [Latin American] countries [the Charter says], the United States is prepared to allocate resources which, along with those anticipated from other external sources, will be of a scope and magnitude adequate to realize the goals envisaged in this Charter.

The United States made this commitment some twenty years after it had begun to extend aid to Latin America. Douglass Cater has referred to it as a "monumental commitment which for size and complexity makes the Marshall Plan look puny by comparison."[1] He did not exaggerate. Unfortunately the American resolve, like the Latin American resolve, has weakened in practice. At least the resolve of the United States Congress, which appropriates the funds with which we support the Alliance, has weakened.

Another instrument of the Alliance has been the Social Progress Trust Fund initiated with a contribution of $525 million supplied by the United States government and first promised by President Eisenhower's representatives at Bogotá. The Social Progress Trust Fund was to be used to provide soft loans and technical assistance to the Latin American countries in the fields of land settlement and improved land use, housing for low-income

1. Douglass Cater, "The Lesson of Punta del Este," *Reporter*, (March 1962), 22.

groups, community water supply and sanitation facilities, and advanced education and training related to economic and social development. The fund was to be used principally to help directly those who most needed help; to make the mass of underprivileged in Latin America more immediately aware of the benefits that the Alliance could bring to them; to enlist them as eager supporters of the Alliance.

The Inter-American Development Bank (IDB), of which the United States and all the other American republics except Cuba are members, also is an important instrument of the Alliance, although it antedates the Alliance by a year and a half. It was to administer the Social Progress Trust Fund.

An additional instrument of development is the Inter-American Committee on the Alliance for Progress, created near the end of 1963. CIAP, as it has come to be called from its initials in Spanish, was given the power to review country plans and the performance of countries and to recommend "the distribution of external funds under the Alliance for Progress." The member states agreed to give special consideration to the recommendations of CIAP. The ostensible reason for setting up CIAP was "to multilateralize" the Alliance. It was hoped that CIAP would play a role similar to that of the OEEC under the Marshall Plan. A 1966 amendment to the Foreign Assistance Act directed that AID (Agency for International Development) loans from Alliance funds must be consistent with CIAP views as determined by its annual country-by-country review of development programs and progress. An unspoken reason for setting up CIAP, of course, was to lift from the United States the burden and the onus of urging and exhorting the Latin American governments to improve their performance under the Alliance, a role that had become as displeasing to the United States as it was to the Latin American governments.

Under Secretary of State Averill Harriman explained CIAP by saying that "it was clear to all that if the Alliance was to fulfill its high expectations, primary responsibility had to be assumed by the governments and people of Latin America . . . Only they have the resources, the knowledge, and the capability of promoting economic growth within the social and political framework they desire." This statement by the under secretary was remarkable only in the sense that it had to be made nearly four years after the

United States had taken the lead in launching the Alliance for Progress.

Of course tax reform and land reform, which our government had insisted on at Bogotá and which are included among the objectives of the Alliance, might also be classified as instruments of development, but until they are enacted and placed in effect and have demonstrated that they are helpful instruments, they remain objectives.

The Alliance's plans for improvement were based on the assumed availability of a supply of capital from all external sources of at least twenty billion dollars, to match an estimated eighty billion dollars of domestic capital during the succeeding ten years. Again reflecting the view of the planners at the Harvard Faculty Club, the twenty billion dollars was to be principally in public funds. Our government agreed that the United States would supply a major portion of those funds. As a matter of fact twenty billion dollars from external sources is by no means an inordinate sum for the Latin American countries to absorb during a ten-year period. Argentina and Brazil, alone, could absorb a very large part of it if they should pursue rational economic policies and create an attractive climate for investment. Given reasonably favorable conditions for investment, the United States would contribute its portion with or without an "Alliance."

The program which the American republics approved in Bogotá in September 1960 was essentially an American program. We had adopted, as our own, ideas of Latin Americans who had impressed our highest officials in Washington, we had added embellishments, and we had sold the ideas back to the Latin American governments as our program. But there was much more of the United States in the Alliance for Progress.

No sooner had our government launched the Alliance upon a sea of oratory than it began to set up small replicas of the Agency for International Development in the various Latin American countries in an effort to help make them over. During a trip I made to Latin America in 1963 I visited ten countries. I found that our Aid missions had grown enormously under the Alliance. When I had resigned as Ambassador to Argentina, three years earlier, the Aid mission in Buenos Aires consisted of six or seven Americans and a handful of local employees. When I visited Buenos Aires in 1963, the number of Americans in the mission had increased to seventy or one hundred and seventy. I don't remember which. In any case, there were many times the number of men who were needed or could be usefully employed.

It seemed to me as I visited the various countries, that for every need a Latin American country had, the United States had sent a technician to meet that need. It mattered little that the country might not have asked for the man and might not even want him. It mattered less that the technician, who probably was an earnest worker in the aid vineyard, might be ignorant of the language of the country where he was to work and of the social and political environment to which he must adjust if his work were to be useful; indeed if it were not to be harmful.

Our Aid Coordinator for Latin America was an energetic leader in the aid effort. He flew up and down the continent, holding press conferences without regard to the views of our ambassadors, bestowing praise on governments here, and censure there, and discussing such politically sensitive subjects as tax reform and land reform with fewer inhibitions than he would have had in his native Puerto Rico. He became such an authority on development in Latin America that he gave ratings to the various countries, much as baseball teams are given ratings in our country. When I flew out of Miami for South America, I read in the Florida papers that Colombia was leading the development league. When I flew into Houston from Guatemala City a month later, Peru had taken over first place and Colombia was in the cellar.

The activists in the Kennedy administration made ringing slogans out of tired clichés. They grasped the Alliance and brandished it as a Kennedy-made torch. How many of them realized that it would have to be a Latin American torch if it were to spark real progress, it is difficult to say.

7. Planning

THE PLANNERS WHO met at Harvard University were confident that government planning would have a leading role in Latin America's economic development. "Such targets as land and tax reform, broader educational opportunities and additional mobilization of domestic capital will become reflected in national programs," they predicted.

President Kennedy, in his White House address to the Latin American diplomats, said,

> If our alliance is to succeed, each Latin nation must formulate long-range plans for its own development—plans which establish targets and priorities, insure monetary stability, establish the machinery for vital social change, stimulate private activity and initiative, and provide for a maximum national effort. These plans will be the foundation of our development effort and the basis for the allocation of outside resources.

Reflecting the president's attitude, the Alliance for Progress provided that participating Latin American governments should formulate long-term plans or programs, if possible within eighteen months, and a panel of "experts," known familiarly as the "nine wise men," was to help in reviewing those programs. The United States government made clear that it would give great importance to the views of the wise men and to those of CIAP, when the latter had, in effect, replaced the wise men.

It is noteworthy in this connection that Chile and Colombia, which together with Brazil are the countries in Latin America where aid is largely concentrated today, have long been known for their skill in drawing up detailed development plans, and their skill in this field undoubtedly has helped them to obtain massive aid from the United States.

In reality of course, Latin American governments, or many of them at least, have long been addicted to drawing up development plans. Chile and Colombia have been unique only in the impressiveness of their efforts. Few Latin American governments have had difficulty drawing up plans. The difficulty has been in carrying them out. The tendency has been to confuse plans with planning. Albert Waterston of the World Bank has said,

> A development plan is not the same as development planning. Those who equate the two—and they are many—confuse what should be—but frequently is not—a product of the planning process for the process itself. Development planning as a process involves the application of a rational system of choices among feasible courses of investment and other development actions based on a consideration of economic and social costs and benefits. Planning as a process is an indispensable precondition for the formulation of effective development policies and measures. A plan can play an important part in the planning process when it makes explicit the basis and rationale for planning policies and measures. But if a plan is prepared before the process has begun in earnest or is unable to generate the process, it is likely to have little significance for development.

I would go a step further than Professor Waterston. I would suggest that such a plan is likely to retard development. By giving a false sense of progress, it reduces opportunities for progress. If underdeveloped countries had the discipline implied in long-term plans; if they were willing and able to adopt the policies needed to carry them out, they wouldn't need plans, although plans that were the result of planning might help them. So far, the most helpful planning in the development field has been embodied in wise decisions—the alteration of a tax rate, the elimination of exchange controls, the offering of incentives to private investment —and it is probable that this will continue to be the case.

Professor Waterston has noted that

a planner cannot do much about a government's administrative inefficiency and its lack of political commitment or will to develop. But if in preparing his plans he ignores these critical factors, which together constitute the main limitations on the ability of most less developed countries to realize their economic possibilities, he ends up by separating his activities and the plans he formulates from the real world outside a national planning agency.[2]

1. Albert Waterston, "What Do We Know about Planning?" *International Development Review,* VII (December 1965).
  2. Ibid.

The long-term plans which the Alliance for Progress sponsored depend for their success on a degree of continuity in the planning process. But continuity in Latin America has been difficult to achieve. The long histories of revolutions and *coups d'état* in most of the Latin American countries are too well known to need recital. It is difficult to exaggerate the disruptive effects of arbitrary and unpredictable change in government. Some arbitrary changes may have brought improvement, as in Brazil in 1964, but in that case improvement was measured against a disastrous economic decline under elected governments. Other arbitrary changes have been less helpful.

Even orderly change frequently cancels out progress already made. More than one Latin American country has been dotted with unfinished schools, hospitals, and dams that governments failed to complete because earlier regimes had started them. In one large country where I served, whose government was seeking a loan from the World Bank to construct new power plants, a Bank study mission reported that the most useful thing the government could do, and the least costly, would be to complete the several power plants begun by earlier governments but abandoned for partisan political reasons. The suggestion aroused no enthusiasm on the part of the government.

Government planning enlarges the area in which political change can have effects. A new administration may not like its predecessors' priorities. It may have its own set of priorities. If history is any criterion, it will. This makes orderly and confident private planning (which is more essential to development than the government plans which the Alliance for Progress has fostered) difficult. And, of course, it makes meaningful government planning difficult too.

It is particularly difficult for Latin American countries to make long-term plans if those plans are based on continuing aid from the United States government, or from any foreign government for that matter, because there can be no assurance that such aid will be available indefinitely, or that it will be available in the amounts planned for. Continuing reductions in foreign aid appropriations by the Congress is evidence of this. Those reductions reflect not only budgetary and balance-of-payments problems in the United States but also a growing disillusionment concerning the results of foreign aid.

But there is another reason the United States government cannot be depended upon to continue aid in ways and in amounts that other countries may plan for, and that is the same tendency we have observed in Latin America for new administrations to act differently from the ways their predecessors have acted. Foreign aid is a political phenomenon more than it is an economic phenomenon, and it is subject to the same uncertainties that other political phenomena are subject to. A new administration in the United States, as in any other country, wants to make a record for itself. This, it usually feels, means doing things differently from the way its predecessors did them, or at least giving the impression it is doing them differently. It wants new programs that will impress people with its dynamism, or if that is not possible, then new names and new images for old programs. What is now the Agency for International Development has had six names since our government went into the aid business systematically.

Seldom have two simple words had so much meaning for so many people as "Point IV." The expression had no planned appeal to people's emotions. It had nothing to do with Madison Avenue. It was not intended to inspire enthusiasm or gratitude. And yet it did both. It conveyed to literally hundreds of millions of people throughout the world whom we were trying to reach, and whom we needed to reach, the simple fact of America's wanting to help. However, when a new administration took over in Washington, it stopped using the expression, and our representatives abroad were discouraged from using it. We threw an inestimable amount of good will and potential for helping people out the window because our government had no enthusiasm for an expression that was associated with an earlier administration.

And of course a new administration feels it needs new men, too. The Administrator of the Agency for International Development, or whatever its current name may be, must be changed. He must be a man who is politically acceptable, if not necessarily technically qualified. Mr. Harold Stassen, when he headed ICA, AID's predecessor organization, introduced the political test even in the appointment and promotion of career officers.

We have seen how the Kennedy administration abruptly expanded our Aid missions in Latin America and the functions alloted to them. It was in the nature of things that those missions would be reduced when they failed to perform the impossible tasks the planners had given them, and that programs would be reduced as well.

Even assuming the capacity of Latin American governments to draw up sensible national programs, possibly with outside help, in few if any of the countries is there a government structure capable of guiding development over a long period. Few Latin American countries have trained civil services capable of carrying on efficiently the conventional services of government, let alone those which leadership and tutelage in the development process would require. Nor in the present state of society and politics in most of the Latin American countries, is it probable that trained civil services will soon emerge. Historically, trained, efficient civil services have emerged from mature societies or have been imposed by mature societies within a colonial relationship. But Latin American societies in general cannot be characterized as mature, and no system of imposing trained civil services on them exists or is recommended by anyone.

8. Reform

WE HAVE HEARD many times in recent years that there are a few persons in the United States with incomes of a million dollars or more who have been paying no federal income tax. That privileged position is alleged by some who enjoy it to reflect certain needs of our economy that are not readily understood by the ordinary taxpayer. But in Latin America the percentage of wealthy who pay minimum taxes has been very high, and there has been little pretense of justifying the privilege on economic grounds.

Wealthy persons in Latin America not only have been subject to very low taxes in the past; a great many of them, as well as a great many less wealthy persons, have been able to evade payment of a large portion of the taxes they were subject to. Tax evasion has not been considered a cardinal sin in Latin America but rather something that "everyone does." In many countries there are few, other than foreigners and foreign firms, who can be depended upon to report earnings fully and to pay on them fairly. This substantial immunity from taxation together with the low wages paid to agricultural workers and domestic servants has enabled the wealthy in Latin America, including some who clamor for more American aid to their countries, to enjoy "gracious living" to a degree no longer possible in the more advanced countries.

The system of land tenure, dating in many countries from enormous grants made to favored families in colonial times, likewise has contributed to gracious living by the wealthy while it has condemned millions of rural workers to virtual serfdom. It also has resulted in underexploitation of agricultural resources, underproduction of foodstuffs, and undernourishment of people. It has been a factor in the general backwardness of most of the Latin American countries.

But inadequate laws governing taxation and land tenure are only a part of Latin America's problems, and of course they are related to all the other factors, some of them deeply ingrained in Latin America's culture. Furthermore, most of those factors are more difficult to change than laws are, and some Latin Americans fear that the effort to change them abruptly is capable of provoking the very political revolution that the proponents of reform claim to be trying to avert. At any rate, the Latin American representatives at the Bogotá conference had little enthusiasm for reform. However, reform had high priority in United States plans for the continent, and the Latin Americans committed themselves to support it, some with tongue in cheek no doubt. It was the price they paid for increased United States aid and, in particular, for the half billion dollar Social Progress Trust Fund, which United States representatives dangled before them.

The planners who met at Harvard University also considered that the need for reform was basic in any effort to promote development in Latin America. In fact the word "reform" was too mild for them. They talked boldly of "revolution" and made clear that they wanted the United States government to have a role in it. "Embarking in partnership upon a social revolution will require action and policies that will appear radical to some and undesirable to others," they warned. But they were far from being deterred by such considerations.

Adopting the planners' view as his own, President Kennedy, in his March 13, 1961, address to Latin American diplomats at the White House, anticipated United States insistence on reform and revolution under the Alliance for Progress when he said, "This political freedom [in Latin America] must be accompanied by social change. For unless necessary social reforms, including land and tax reforms, are freely made—then our alliance, our revolution, our dream, and our freedom will fail."

It was in the nature of things therefore that the Alliance for Progress pledged that its signatories would work

To encourage, in accordance with the characteristics of each country, programs of comprehensive agrarian reform, leading to the effective transformation, where required, of unjust structures and systems of land tenure and use; with a view to replacing latifundia and dwarf holdings by an equitable system of property so that, supplemented by timely and adequate credit, technical assistance and improved marketing arrangements, the land will become for the man who works it the basis of his economic stability, the foundation of his increasing welfare, and the guarantee of his freedom and dignity.

The signatories also agreed "to reform tax laws, demanding more from those who have most, to punish tax evasion severely, and to redistribute the national income in order to benefit those who are most in need, while at the same time, promoting savings and investment and reinvestment of capital."

High officials of the Kennedy administration, including some who were close to the president, were especially reform-minded. They were convinced not only of the need of reform but of the urgency of the United States government's playing an aggressive role in bringing it about.

AID representatives in Latin America were encouraged to press for reform, and some did so with enthusiasm. In one South American capital that I visited in 1963 I talked to the Aid Director about the changes I had noted since an earlier visit there. "There have been changes," he said grudgingly, "but not enough. You see, this country hasn't had its revolution yet." It was clear from his attitude that he thought the country should have its revolution soon and that he wanted to take part in it.

Even ambassadors were rated by the degree to which the governments that they were accredited to enacted reform, sometimes without reference to whether the governments had acted under pressure from the ambassador or on their own.

Many persons in the Congress, perhaps intrigued by the thought that reform would bring progress to Latin America and an end to the need of costly aid programs in the area, also supported reform and revolution in Latin America. In a report to the Committee on Foreign Relations dated April 13, 1963, the then Senator Hubert H. Humphrey said,

In all the areas encompassed by the Alliance—agriculture, business, education—we must ask ourselves: Are we truly ready for the changes that we are encouraging? Are we ready for the changes that may very well temporarily cause a flight of capital because of the change in tax laws; changes that will bring into government the more inexperienced and radical elements in the social structure; changes that will basically alter land ownership and laws pertaining to investment: These are just a few of the changes that we should expect in any kind of democratic revolution that we seem to be encouraging. I believe that we can tolerate these changes and that in the long run they will represent progress. But we need to condition the American public to tolerate some of the excesses that will accompany the accomplishment of these changes. We must be prepared to bend to the tide of nationalism that is sweeping over the Western Hemisphere, and to give some leeway to the friendly governments who are being pressured by the left or by the extreme right.

Please note that Mr. Humphrey, who at the time would probably have yielded to few persons in certainty concerning what is needed to bring about progress in Latin America, was not worried about whether the Latin Americans could tolerate the changes we were encouraging. He took for granted that private capital would find it difficult to tolerate some of those changes, since he contemplated a flight of capital from the area. True, for reasons he did not divulge, he seemed certain that the flight of capital would be temporary, presumably not long enough to plunge countries into the economic and social chaos that might create opportunities for new Castros. In any case he was quite ready to face that danger and whatever other dangers the revolution should bring to Latin America, even though many Latin Americans might not be. What did concern him was whether the American public, who of course elect senators and support or condone votes for foreign aid, were willing to face them.

Latin American politicians, particularly those who represent what the Senator called "the more inexperienced and radical elements in the social structure," were doubtless delighted at Mr. Humphrey's words, which offered hope that the United States government would compensate for the losses they might cause their countries' economies. But more than one Latin American whose cooperation in bringing about development was needed must have wondered, when he read the Senator's words, what new and strange kind of imperialism the United States was embarked upon in the name of the Alliance for Progress.

A report to the Committee on Foreign Relations, U.S. Senate, on the second Punta del Este Conference, which was held in January 1962, to consider the case of Castro Cuba, says,

One of the reasons U.S. prestige has increased in Latin America in the last 18 months is that, beginning with President Eisenhower's statement of July 11, 1960, foreshadowing the Act of Bogotá and the Alianza para el Progreso, the United States has moved to dissociate itself from the extreme conservatives at the top of the Latin American oligarchies. This element is out of sympathy with every current U. S. policy except anti-Castroism. Its days as a political influence in Latin America are numbered. It will either be overthrown by a Castro-type revolution, or it will be pushed aside by the kind of peaceful revolution envisaged by the Alianza para el Progreso. Although the members of this element proclaim themselves the real friends of the United States, they are not in fact. If the United States once again identifies itself with those elements, it will lose the good chance it now has to win the friendship of the rising liberal forces who are going to determine the future of Latin America, either through democratic processes or through a Castroist perversion.

The signers of the report are Senator Wayne Morse, a Democrat who frequently backed liberal causes, and Senator Bourke D. Hickenlooper, a Republican who, despite the harsh words he had for the "extreme conservatives" in Latin America, was a supporter, in the United States, of the presidential candidacy of Barry Goldwater.

Senator Hickenlooper did some rethinking of his position with reference to what he called "the rising liberal forces in Latin America." The Hickenlooper amendment to the Foreign Assistance Act prohibits American aid to governments that have expropriated American property without arranging for prompt and effective compensation to the owners. In reply to Mr. Humphrey's question as to whether we can tolerate the changes we have been encouraging in Latin America and the excesses that will accompany some of them, the Senator from Iowa, and a majority of Congress, after having thought it over, answered, "No, we can't."

Reform in Latin America did not begin with the Act of Bogotá or the Alliance for Progress, as many commentators seem to imply. On the contrary, most governments in Latin America have presented themselves as "reform" governments. Furthermore, if reform consisted of putting laws on the books, Latin America already would be one of the most reformed areas in the world. The difficulty has not been in promising reform or enacting it. It has been in making reform work. That difficulty still has to be overcome.

9. The Alliance and Foreign Private Capital

ALTHOUGH THE planners who met at the Harvard Faculty Club emphasized the importance of public investment in spurring development, they also paid tribute to the role of private investment. In their report to President-elect Kennedy they said,

As with public investment, these objectives will not be achieved unless private investment is accorded a major and expanding role. In U.S. society, the human and organizational resources at the command of private enterprise provide the crucial margin in our national capacity to assist Latin America achieve full economic and social modernization. The contribution of private investment is not merely monetary capital or the production of more goods at lower costs. . . . It carries with it more than indispensable production know-how and improved methods of management and industrial relations. It can also impart broadened opportunities for closer human ties of sympathy and understanding which are basic elements in the new, joint adventure in partnership. A major effort must, therefore, be directed toward the creation of a better understanding of the capacity of private investment for crucial contributions on virtually all fronts of the new Alliance for Progress. While we recognize that there exists in Latin America some prejudice against private investment—particularly against foreign investment—we would be remiss if we did not support those elements of leadership which realize and seek these contributions.

Within the multilateral relationships discussed later, we must undertake to create a more receptive attitude to foreign investment by the governments and people of Latin America.

One of the authors of the Harvard Clearing House Report is Professor Lincoln Gordon. President Kennedy named Professor Gordon his ambassador to Brazil. Later the professor was brought to Washington to serve as Assistant Secretary of State for Latin America and United States Coordinator for the Alliance for Progress. While he was in Brazil Professor Gordon published a book entitled, A New Deal for Latin America: The Alliance for Progress, in which he stated,

A careful reading of the Charter of Punta del Este shows that private enterprise has a role of primary importance. It is the main source of initiative and of action in the development of industry, agriculture, finance, commerce, and distribution. A major purpose of the over-all developmental planning so strongly emphasized by the Charter is to provide a framework of institutions and incentives to encourage the most rapid possible expansion of constructive private enterprise and to ensure that an adequate share of the total resources for investment will be available for use by the private sector.[1]

It is true that one of the objectives of the Alliance for Progress, as set forth in the Declaration of Punta del Este, was "to stimulate private enterprise in order to encourage the development of Latin American countries at a rate which will help them to provide jobs for their growing populations, to eliminate unemployment, and to take their place among the modern industrialized nations of the world." It is true that the Charter itself contains several references to private enterprise. But, as Professor Gordon suggests, it takes careful reading to find them.

In any event, once the Alliance was in effect Professor Gordon appeared to doubt that government planning, which the Charter called for with insistence, was having the effect of stimulating private enterprise, either domestic or foreign. In a warning clearly addressed to the Latin American governments, he went on to say in his book

This form of planning for development does not mean centralized control of the whole economic structure on totalitarian lines. It means planning that is concentrated on two essential elements: (1) an integrated program of public investment in economic and social infrastructure for which government has direct responsibility, with assured financing on a non-inflationary basis, and (2) provision of a framework of institutions and incentives within which private enterprise can function efficiently. The government development plans, in a sense, may be likened to the arteries of a healthy human being, with

---

1. Lincoln Gordon, *A New Deal for Latin America: The Alliance for Progress,* (Cambridge, Mass., 1963), p. 84.

private enterprise providing the blood cells which flow through those arteries.[2]

The Professor was describing a kind of ideal state. But many persons intimately familiar with Latin America are skeptical that the ideal state will soon emerge in that area. They fear, rather, that if the "blood cells" of private enterprise are expected to flow through the "arteries" of government planning then many Latin American economies will continue in their present state of anaemia, unless, of course, new and more successful efforts are made to insure that the blood is richer and more plentiful than it now is, and the hardening process that tends to attack government arteries in Latin America is reversed.

The gap between the developed countries and the countries of Latin America is widening rapidly. Alliance supporters hope that the widening process can be slowed down, but it is difficult to see how that can be accomplished without the help of new foreign private capital and of techniques that are principally in foreign private hands. And yet, many Latin American countries have made only half-hearted efforts to attract foreign private capital. The policies of some have served rather to repel new capital as well as to antagonize capital that is already in the country.

Professor John Pincus has pointed out a basic dilemma in the problem of attracting new private investment to the less developed countries. The dilemma applies to Latin America as well as to other areas. According to Professor Pincus

The Foreign private investment problem in North-South relations can perhaps best be characterized as a case of dual schizophrenia. The South has ideological objections to foreign direct investment, but a material need for it, as one catalyst of growth. The North has an ideological preference for private investment as an agent of growth, but no great material need to invest in developing countries. The result is predictable. The North preaches the virtues of private investment, but does most of its foreign investing in industrial countries—venturing elsewhere primarily in search of minerals. The South plays a balancing game, simultaneously trying to attract foreign investors by model legislation and frightening them away by a formidable combination of controls and expressions of hostility, the latter

2. *Ibid.*, p. 84.

usually coinciding with election campaigns or other periods of domestic political disarray.[3]

He also notes that

> Rates of return for foreign investment in most developing countries are usually not very high compared with alternative uses of capital. When this fact is coupled with risk considerations, investment in Less Developed Countries is hardly enticing. Each side then tends to think that he is playing a cat-and-mouse game. But there are, to borrow a luminous phrase, two cats and no mice.[4]

A major tragedy in Latin America is the steady emigration abroad, principally to the United States, of persons with education and skills that the countries require if they are to progress. This "brain drain" parallels a similar drain of dollars that Latin Americans send abroad for investment and safekeeping. Together they serve to negate much of the effort the government of the United States and the international agencies are making to support development in Latin America.

In theory, the educated and skilled people who emigrate to other countries, if they remained in Latin America, would help to insure the progress to which the area aspires. However, while skills promote development they also require a degree of development, a certain momentum in the development process, before they can be used effectively. An industrial manager needs a plant to manage. A scientist needs a laboratory and a project that is adequately financed. Foreign private capital can add to the momentum of development, but its help frequently is spurned by governments for nationalistic and demagogic reasons.

3. John Pincus, *Trade, Aid and Development: The Rich and Poor Nations,* (New York, 1967), p. 359.
4. *Ibid.,* p. 360.

10. Accomplishments of the Alliance

WHAT HAVE BEEN the accomplishments of the Alliance for Progress? They are not easy to measure, especially since the roots of many of them antedate the Alliance. If the Alliance succeeds, many of its accomplishments will not be evident for years. But neither will all its shortcomings be immediately apparent.

There is a temptation on the part of the Alliance's detractors to conclude that because some of the wildly optimistic predictions of progress the Alliance would bring have not been met, the Alliance has brought no progress to Latin America. There is an equal temptation on the part of its supporters to give credit to the Alliance for all gains that the Latin American countries have made during the last eight years, including improved weather on the Argentine pampa. Some supporters give the impression that development in Latin America began the day the Charter of Punta del Este was signed. Some suggest that reform and revolution were introduced into Latin America by President Eisenhower and his brother, Milton, or later by President Kennedy and his White House assistants. Some talk as though there had been no program of American aid to Latin America prior to the Alliance.

Because many of the Alliance's proponents in the United States discovered Latin America only after a mob had insulted Vice-President Nixon on the streets of Lima, some of them assume that the government of the United States also has discovered it only recently. There is of course no way of knowing how many of the gains that Latin America may have made under the Alliance would have been made without an Alliance, or whether total gain might not have been greater if the Alliance had not been formed.

In any event the Alliance's achievements have been amply publicized in speeches of political leaders in the United States and in the reports of the United States agency that administers aid. Readers of those reports would do well to bear in mind, however, that their principal purpose is to justify new appropriations by the United States Congress, and that in order to succeed in that purpose, facts presented must be carefully selected so that neither will progress be downgraded nor need minimized.

In his 1966 report to the Congress AID Administrator, David E. Bell, noted that

> In physical terms, well over half the people of Latin America are benefitting from U.S.-assisted alliance programs, including more than 25 million who are receiving surplus food from the United States and 100 million people who are protected from malaria through U.S.-supported eradication programs. More than 1.5 million people are living in Alliance sponsored homes; a million children are attending school for the first time because of new Alliance class-rooms; hundreds of thousands of people are receiving medical attention from new hospitals and health centers; and more than 13 million people are benefitting from Alliance-financed water supply and sanitation projects.

He goes on to say

> The credit needs of private individuals and corporations have been recognized and are beginning to be met. The United States has authorized loans of more than $440 million to intermediate credit institutions and cooperatives in 18 nations, and to the Central American Bank for Economic Integration. In six countries there are more than 1,300 credit unions with 358,000 members and savings of more than $15 million. Through aid assistance to intermediate credit institutions, more than 350,000 farmers have received agricultural credit loans. Nineteen development banks have been established. The United States has made loans totalling more than $17 million in support of these.

These are important achievements, and Mr. Bell also named others. But in relation to need, total progress has been small. In some areas there has been retrogression. Mr. Bell continued,

> The Alliance has awakened Latin America to the magnitude of the challenge of development, but poverty is still the lot of the majority of the people. . . . Despite progress in home construction, the number of ill-housed people is increasing. Despite greater attention to education, the percentage of school-age children attending school is not increasing; in fact the percentage of illiterates may be growing.

For all the efforts of the Alliance, unemployment remains a crushing problem. In several countries, inflation saps the incentive to save. Budget deficits continue. Poorly operated public enterprises are contributing to government imbalance. Monopolistic practices and regressive tax structures restrict the development of national markets.

The situation Mr. Bell described persists today.

Two years after Mr. Bell had made his report a new AID Administrator, Mr. William S. Gaud, made these references to area-wide progress:

A distinct trend to more stable and more numerous representative governments, coupled with increasing readiness of political leadership to make and support decisions essential to development, is evident in the Latin America of 1967.

The increasing engagement of all levels of Latin American society in the vast work of development is another mark of forward movement under the Alliance for Progress. So is the expanding concensus that economic integration of Latin America is an important key to sounder and more rapid growth.

Although large and often intractable problems still confront the region, progress under the Alliance and the steady increase in constructive attitudes it has engendered are testimony to the soundness of the Alliance idea and to the vigor with which it has been pursued in the face of difficulties.

Later he noted that

A further index of favorable change in Latin America is the growth of middle-class recognition of its pivotal role in economic development. For it is this social segment that is furnishing the technicians who are increasing farmland production, starting small and medium industries, improving marketing procedures, organizing cooperatives, building power, transport and communications systems, or extending the reach of education and public health programs. Such people are the key to greater Latin American capacity for effective absorption of the larger amounts of external help the region will require.

The gains Mr. Gaud mentioned, if they are lasting, are important and even basic. But they are hard to put a finger on in the climate of unpredictable political and economic fluctuation that still characterizes so much of Latin American society. The trend toward stable and more representative government, for example, is difficult to discern.

In more concrete terms Mr. Gaud observed that "Brazil's stabilization campaign . . . has reduced its rate of price increases from an annual rate of 140 percent in early 1964 to 41 percent in 1966. Chile's inflation spiral, which in 1964 took prices up 40 percent, was held to a 17 percent rise in 1966. Uruguay managed to reduce inflation from 88 percent in 1965 to under 50 percent in 1966." Gains in the perpetual war against inflation are particularly hard to put a finger on. They tend often to be ephemeral. In any case the gains Mr. Gaud referred to indicate less how good the situation was in 1967 than how bad it had been earlier. They illustrate the extremely low base from which improvement in Latin America continues to be measured.

Mr. Gaud included steps toward economic integration in Latin America as an Alliance accomplishment. Latin America's efforts at integration antedate the Alliance. Furthermore the United States initially gave little support to Latin American integration. However it now supports the movement with measured enthusiasm.

The Central American Common Market (CACM) has had substantial success in increasing trade among countries of the area. On the other hand the Latin American Free Trade Area (LAFTA), comprising ten South American countries and Mexico, is progressing only slowly and painfully. Vested interests, private and governmental, hinder real integration and probably make it remote. As an example, the highly protected automobile manufacturing industry in the LAFTA countries, built up principally since 1957, is already ten times larger than the market justifies and continues to expand.[1] Real integration would require the closure of plants rather than their further expansion, but this does not fit in with the plans of member governments.

Mr. Gaud pointed out in his report that Latin American investment under the Alliance for Progress has exceeded expectations, "Latin American investment stands at about 17 percent of total gross national product and in the last three years has increased faster. At this rate, even allowing for price increases, total investment over the "Decade of Development" will far exceed the $100 billion envisioned at Punta del Este in 1961. Gross annual investment, computed at 1965 prices, has reached $16

1. Jack Baranson, "Integrated Automobiles in Latin America?" *Finance and Development*, No. 4 (1968), 25.

billion." This is good news if the estimate is accurate and if most of the investment is economic.

Nevertheless, Mr. Gaud said, "the challenge remains." He summarized a part of the challenge in this way,

The most basic obstacle to economic and social development in Latin America is its population growth rate of nearly three per cent annually, highest in the world. If present trends continue the population of Alliance countries will double every 24 years and reach 625 million by the year 2000. Over 40 percent of the present population, estimated at 237 million in 1966, is below the age of 15, a fact that foreshadows vastly expanded demands on Latin economies.

The staggering challenge is partially indicated by the following: "Farm production should rise by six percent every year, double the present rate.

"At least 140 million new jobs must be created in the remainder of the century.

"Over a million new homes will be needed annually merely to match population growth.

"More than 200,000 more physicians will be needed by 1980 simply to maintain the present wholly inadequate ratio of doctors to people.

"Hundreds of thousands of new classrooms are required simply to meet minimum standards by 1970.

"If Latin American economies are to meet these needs, annual percapita gross national product growth rates should increase to from 3.5 to 4 percent rather than the original 2.5 percent target of the Alliance."

It is evident that officials in Washington have striven manfully to demonstrate that United States aid to Latin America has contributed to progress in the area, but that the task is a difficult one. To many observers it appears that after more than twenty-five years of United States aid Latin America as a whole is on a treadmill, and that despite efforts that are impressive, or that appear impressive in a certain light, it remains in the same place or even a few steps behind the point where it found itself the day the Alliance for Progress was signed. That feeling is increasingly shared by the United States Congress, which of course appropriates or withholds funds for foreign aid.

When Assistant Secretary of State Lincoln Gordon, who also was United States Coordinator for the Alliance for Progress, made his final appearance before a Congressional Subcommittee to request additional funds for the 1968 Alliance program the following exchange took place:

Mr. Gordon: "To conclude, I hesitate to make prophecies, but perhaps as a departing official of the Government in this field I may indulge in one. As I see the situation today, there is still a very long and hard road ahead in the development of Latin America and its transformation into a series of truly modern societies with democratic political stability and self-sustained economic growth. After 6 years of the Alliance for Progress, I think we can say with real confidence that the course of the hemisphere is set in the right direction, and if the summit decisions can be fully implemented, I think there is a very good chance of keeping it set in the right direction. In fact, I would say when historians of the future look back on this period, they will look on the Alliance for Progress as one of the really great turning points in the evolution of the hemisphere and, therefore, in the evolution or world affairs, a turning point of very great long term interest to the United States.

"Now, what has been accomplished in these 6 years has been made possible because this committee and the Congress have given it sustained support.

"President Johnson said on the 14th. of April, upon leaving Punta del Este to return home, and I quote his words, 'Development is a task not for sprinters, but for long distance runners.' "

Mr. [Congressman] Passman: "Thank you, Mr. Secretary. We have a very high regard for you personally. You have been a dedicated public servant.

"The achievements of the past have been so far short of our expectations or goals that I question whether I should comment on what you are presently prophesying.

"I believe, though, Mr. Secretary, when you appeared before this committee some 6 years ago, you were testifying for a 10-year program. . . . Over half of that time has elapsed and it seems that we are just a few feet away from the starting gate. I hope your prophecies for the future can be more accurate, insofar as time and money are concerned, than they have been in the past. I say that simply because we will have to live with this program for many years no doubt after you have departed.

"I think that you would agree that profound statements, pretty phrases, imagination, wishing, and dreaming is one thing, but the realities of life are something entirely different, aren't they?"

Mr. Gordon: "Yes, sir, I would comment that I think we are a great deal more than a few feet from the gate."

Mr. Passman: "I think we are still in sight of where we started over 6 years ago."[2]

Representative Passman, over the years, has been a severe and constant critic of the foreign aid program. Nevertheless opinion in the Congress has moved steadily in the direction of the view he expressed. In a sense, of course, Congressman Passman's view is moderate. It is possible to go beyond what he said and take the view not that progress under the Alliance has been slight but that no overall progress has been made; that problems in Latin America are greater than when the Alliance was launched, with no clear solutions in sight.

Why have the Alliance for Progress, and the extraordinary effort the United States government has made within the Alliance, not been more productive? In searching for possible answers it would be well to examine the nature of the phenomenon we call aid.

Aid is an instrument of diplomacy, and diplomacy is a frustrating exercise, even for its most expert practitioners. Its success depends in large measure on inducing foreigners to act in ways that we think are desirable. Charles Burton Marshall, in his classical study, *The Limits of Foreign Policy*, has said,

The fundamental circumstance giving rise to foreign policy is that most of the world is outside the United States. The areas in which our foreign policy has its effects are those lying beyond the range of our law. They include about fifteen-sixteenths of the world's land surface and contain about sixteen-seventeenths of its peoples. We cannot ordain the conditions there. The forces do not respond to our fiat. At best we can only affect them. We exercise only influence, not the sovereign power to dispose, in those ranges once described by the Supreme Court in a memorable opinion as "this vast external realm, with its important, complicated, delicate and manifold problems."

We cannot legislate for foreign countries, although the Congress, when it approves foreign assistance acts, may have the illusion that it is doing that. We cannot order foreign peoples to adhere to policies that we think are wise or to act in ways that we think are desirable.

2. U.S., Congress, House, Subcommittee of the Committee on Appropriations, *Hearing on Foreign Operations and Related Agencies: Economic Assistance*, 90th Cong., 1st sess., 1968, pp. 1198–99, pt. 2.

Aid is a particularly frustrating exercise in diplomacy. Aid to the underdeveloped countries involves not only changing people's minds in connection with specific matters and issues, but changing people themselves. That is its principal objective in many cases. That is basically what it is all about.

There are two kinds of resources on which countries can build to achieve development—material resources and human resources, and of the two, human resources are by far the more important. Most countries receiving aid from the United States are new countries with little experience in meeting the problems of nationhood. But the Latin American countries are not new countries. They have been independent more than a century and a half. They do not lack experience in meeting problems. They lack success in meeting them. At least success, in their case, has not been commensurate with need.

Economic and social problems in many Latin American countries are becoming more rather than less difficult. As populations have grown, people's needs have become greater and their demands more insistent. Agriculture is providing employment to a decreasing percentage of a rapidly increasing population. Even the smallest country has become industrialized to a degree, and aspires to become more industrialized. Unfortunately no equivalent emphasis is placed on agriculture, which tends to be associated in the minds of people, and especially of governments, with a less industrialized, less dynamic, and less glamorous past, which Latin Americans would like to leave behind.

Coffee and other traditional products that can be sold abroad for dollars and pounds are produced with varying degrees of enthusiasm. But countries with very low living standards and enormous agricultural potential are spending scarce foreign exchange for imported foodstuffs. In contrast to a highly industrialized United States, which also accounts for 20 percent of the world's agricultural output, although it has only 6 percent of the world's population, Latin America's agricultural production, already inadequate, is growing less rapidly than its population.

Nor has industrialization proceeded at the pace Latin Americans hoped it would, and that necessity requires. Literally millions of country people whom the land can no longer support have drifted to cities looking for jobs. Unable to obtain them, many huddle together in shantytowns where they live off the cities' excrement. In Lima, Santiago, Buenos Aires and Rio de Janeiro those *callampas*, *favelas*, and *villas miseria* offer a stark and startling contrast to the conspicuous opulence of the overprivileged.

Aid depends for its success on people acting rationally and cooperatively, and our government's plans in the aid field, like the national development plans we have encouraged the other American republics to draw up, are based on the assumption that they will do that. But if the people we are trying to help could be depended upon to act rationally and cooperatively, they wouldn't need as much help from foreign governments as they do now. They would be able to solve their problems with a minimum of what we call aid. And if we had the ability to act rationally and cooperatively to the degree required, our help would be more effective. Success for our aid program in Latin America will come from improved performance on both sides. How can that be achieved? Before we address ourselves to that question it would be well to look at the environment in which the program operates.

THE AID ENVIRONMENT

---

11. Revolution of Rising Expectations

SEVERAL YEARS AGO a young and earnest friend of mine asked me how it seemed to watch a revolution of rising expectations. It was evident that he had in mind a modern version of the French Revolution, with men and women and children marching and singing and brandishing pitchforks and other useful utensils. I told my friend that I had never seen a revolution of rising expectations, although I had lived in so-called underdeveloped countries a great part of my life. I said, however, that I had read a great deal about the subject in the New York *Times* and in the writings of Adlai Stevenson.

When aid seemed to hold more promise than it does now, there was a great deal of talk about the revolution of rising expectations. Today less is heard about it. Is the phrase, revolution of rising expectations, an accurate one and a useful one? Is it self-fulfilling in a sense? Is there a revolution of rising expectations going on now?

It seems to me that there is something that may be called a revolution of rising expectations, even though the expression is capable of misleading as well as enlightening. In this day of rapid communication, of the motion picture, the television, the airplane, and the ubiquitous and free-spending American tourist, people in the less developed countries are bound to be more acutely conscious than they used to be of differences between their living standards and standards in the more highly developed countries. And if one adds the effects of countless books, articles, and speeches by political leaders and political scientists, particularly in the United States where development and aid have become emotional as well as economic themes, and if one also adds the utterances of political leaders in the less developed countries who quote and embroider upon what our political leaders and our scholars have said, it would indeed be surprising if expectations, or hopes at least, for material improvement had not risen in the minds of many in the less developed countries.

Undoubtedly there were high expectations in the former colonies of the great European powers when they assumed a free though still unequal status among the nations of the world—a kind of euphoria perhaps, a naïve assumption that national independence, together with aid from the more developed countries, would bring abrupt improvement in living standards. But those expectations must to some extent have been diminished by experience.

And in the less developed countries that have been long independent, which have been able to identify themselves with the former colonies as equally entitled to aid, in part through a tortured claim of having themselves been "economic" colonies up to now, there must have been somewhat higher hopes for improvement after aid became a normal part of our diplomacy.

Our aid programs in Latin America were started during World War II. Did the revolution of rising expectations in Latin America, to the extent it may exist, begin with those programs? Or with President Truman's Point IV Program, which had great emotional impact throughout the world? Or did it begin with the dramatically successful Marshall Plan and an equally tortured identification of the Latin American countries with the highly advanced countries of Europe that were the Plan's beneficiaries?

It was not only Latin Americans who identified their countries with Europe as equally entitled to massive aid. President Kennedy himself drew the analogy in unmistakable terms. In his March 13, 1961, address to the Latin American diplomats proposing an Alliance for Progress, the president said,

Thus, if the countries of Latin America are ready to do their part—and I am sure they are—then I believe the United States, for its part, should help provide resources of a scope and magnitude sufficient to make this bold development plan a success, just as we helped to provide, *against nearly equal odds*, the resources adequate to help rebuild the economies of Western Europe. (italics added)

When President Kennedy made that statement, of course, he knew very little about Latin America or its people. Similarly many of those who have talked most of the revolution of rising expectations have had little acquaintance with the people who they allege are embarked on the revolution, or with the circumstances in which those people live. Was the change as much in those who discovered the revolution as it was in those who were purported to be carrying it out? Was the phenomenon new to the new and instant experts rather than new in itself?

There has been an economic and social revolution going on in Mexico, but it started more than fifty years ago. It has had a good measure of success. The United States government may have given the revolution an assist by adopting an understanding attitude toward the Mexican government's expropriation of American petroleum properties, although who can say with confidence that the revolution would not have progressed faster if the companies had been permitted to continue to help Mexico develop its petroleum resources, leaving the Mexican government free to apply its own resources to other urgent needs of the nation? More than fifty years after the revolution began, living standards in Mexico still are low. Aside from that assist, if it was one, from the government of the United States, and some superlative aid from the Rockefeller Foundation in the agricultural field, Mexico has carried out its revolution nearly entirely with its own resources and, in recent years, with increasing help from foreign private capital. Aid from the government of the United States has been minimal.

Is the Mexican revolution a revolution of rising expectations? If it is then the phenomenon is not as new in Latin America as it is often presented as being.

Some six thousand persons were killed in tiny El Salvador, in 1933, in a revolution that lasted only a few days. Unlike the later Cuban revolution, the Salvadoran revolution was carried out chiefly by peasants who were fighting for land and other benefits for themselves. It was close to the model of revolution of rising expectations that my friend had in mind. The Salvadoran revolution failed and it has not since been repeated, in the same form at least. There were only meager reports about it at the time. The world press was little interested in Latin America or in the other less developed areas. Nor were the scholars much interested. Few persons outside El Salvador know today that the revolution occurred. Many Salvadorans have forgotten it. Was it a revolution of rising expectations? It happened thirty-six years ago.

There may have been a revolution of frustrated expectations in Colombia in 1948. The Colombian masses that year had well-founded reasons to complain about the conditions in which they lived, and against the privileged classes who controlled the country's economy. They had had reason to complain from the time the Spaniards took over the country, seized its rich valleys, and forced the indigenous population to move to the hillsides, where many of the dispossessed still live and still have great difficulty scratching out a meager existence from the soil. Their cause for complaint may have been greater in 1948 than it had been two centuries before because a poorly clothed, ill-housed and ill-nourished urban proletariat had added its woes to those of the hill dwellers.

On April 9, 1948, Dr. Jorge Eliecer Gaitan, a dynamic leader of Colombia's Liberal Party, was assassinated in Bogotá, the nation's capital. Gaitan had promised to lead Colombia's masses out of the poverty and distress in which they lived, and many had placed their faith in him. When he was assassinated, the city of Bogotá erupted. A very large part of its population, and an additional horde who invaded the city from the surrounding hills, rose up against the existing order of things. A thousand persons were killed in the city in a few days. Downtown Bogotá was largely destroyed. The home of Simon Bolivar, Colombia's most revered hero, was burned. The home of President Mariano Ospina Perez was surrounded and attacked. Terror took possession of Bogotá.

The Bogotazo, as it came to be known, occurred while the Ninth International Conference of American States was meeting at Bogotá. The United States delegation was headed by Secretary of State George C. Marshall. Latin America was represented by some of its most distinguished statesmen. Most of them had a single overriding purpose that they hoped to accomplish in Bogotá—to convince Secretary Marshall of the need of a Marshall Plan for Latin America. The occasion seemed especially propitious. Expectations of Latin American political leaders were high.

But early in the Conference Secretary Marshall announced, publicly and clearly, that there would be no Marshall Plan for Latin America. The Secretary and other members of the American delegation explained patiently that United States resources were not unlimited and that, furthermore, problems in Latin America were not the same problems that existed in Europe and would not yield to the same treatment. They pointed out that the Marshall Plan was serving Latin America's interest as well as the interest of Europe and the United States. It would open the way to the return of a viable and secure free world. It would help save Latin America as well as other areas from economic and social chaos, and possibly from political chaos as well. It would give all free countries the opportunity to progress in peace.

Secretary Marshall made his announcement that there would be no Marshall Plan for Latin America before the Bogotazo occurred, and the Colombian people heard him. But there was no popular reaction, no bitterness. While some political leaders might have harbored resentment, none was shown by the Colombian man on the street. If the Colombian masses were engaged in a revolution of rising expectations they gave no evidence at Bogotá that the revolution was directed in any way against the United States.

The reaction of Colombians to Gaitan's assassination was spontaneous and massive. Bogotá's streets were quickly choked with an angry multitude that looted and burned and killed those who placed themselves in its way. It has not been established that the Communists were responsible for Gaitan's assassination or for most of the events that followed. What is clear is that they took prompt advantage of the uprising and made strenuous efforts to lead it. Organized squads of rioters and arsonists appeared on the streets minutes after the assassination. Communist groups quickly and expertly seized the radio stations and began to harangue the mob that filled the streets. They tried to direct the mob against the Americans whom they charged with responsibility for Gaitan's death.

There was little that Americans could have done to defend themselves in the situation. Secretary Marshall had five Colombian soldiers, all young recruits, guarding him. The army contingents normally stationed in the area were away on maneuvers, and the Bogotá police had joined the mob and delivered their weapons over to them. But Secretary Marshall needed no defense. No hostile person came near him. The American Ambassador, seeking his way to the embassy offices in downtown Bogotá, found himself in the middle of a drunken mob. But no one laid a hand on him or addressed an unfriendly word to him. I know because I was the Ambassador.

Colombians, rightly or wrongly, blamed their own government and the privileged classes who controlled the country's economy for the misery they were suffering and that Gaitan had promised to alleviate. Only the Communists pointed the finger of blame toward the United States. The mass of Colombians ignored them.

Of course the Bogotazo occurred more than twenty years ago and the temper of the world was not what it became later. There was little talk of a revolution of rising expectations. Perhaps the phrase had not yet been coined. There was no assumption that the United States was responsible for the failures of other nations as well as for its own failures. There was little breast-beating by United States government officials, little tendency to believe that the sixteen-seventeenths of the world that lives outside the United States would quickly solve its grievous problems if only we in the United States would act differently.

Is there a Latin American revolution of rising expectations today? Possibly there is. There is at least the remnant of one in the press, particularly in the American press, and in the speeches of some American and Latin American political leaders. Perhaps it is principally there. Certainly if there is such a revolution, our government has done much to encourage it, even though it may have been able, so far, to do little to make it succeed.

12. "Economic Imperialism"

Today's students of aid, and many of their teachers, have known no other world than one in which systematic, large-scale aid by the governments of developed countries to the governments and people of underdeveloped countries is a normal feature of international relations, and they therefore have no basis in experience from which to compare today's world with yesterday's pre-aid world. Those students and teachers must have to remind themselves frequently that despite the great importance given to aid by economists, political scientists, and persons in government, all but a tiny portion of the material and social progress that has taken place in the world has been achieved in the absence of what we call aid.

There were no aid programs as such when I entered the Foreign Service in the early 1920's. Latin Americans, in general, would have been suspicious of any effort by the government of the United States to "interfere" in their domestic affairs by subsidizing governments or sectors of the population, or by preaching "reform," especially in politically sensitive areas. Their attitude would have differed little from the attitude we would take today if a foreign government should indulge in such tactics in our country.

Foreign nations in the 1920's extended economic cooperation to the countries of Latin America through the medium of private enterprise, largely through direct investment by private firms. Many of the foreign investors were American. In some countries they were principally American. Foreign investments were largely in the extractive industries: in petroleum production, the mining of copper and silver, lead and zinc, and of nitrates; and in large-scale, plantation-type agriculture and the processing of agricultural products. Production was mostly for export.

These industries played important roles in the economies of the countries where they were located and in supporting the public treasuries. Few of them would have existed if foreigners had not been willing to invest in them and manage them. At least they would not have existed on the same large scale. Most of the industries continue to make important contributions to the economies of the Latin American countries. Some of them are the mainstay of those economies and have been for many years. Power companies and other utilities also were largely foreign owned, and there was foreign investment in manufacturing, although it was small in comparison with later investment in that field.

Foreign banks and banking firms took care of Latin America's need for external credit. Money moved across political frontiers with a minimum of interference from governments. If a Latin American government wanted a loan from abroad to finance a public works program, or for whatever other purpose, it applied to a New York banking firm, or perhaps to a London firm, and frequently it got the loan. The cooperation that private United States sources extended to Latin America was welcomed in that area. What Latin America wanted from abroad were resources it lacked: capital, equipment and other assets, and techniques, and all these were available from private sources and were supplied by them. Furthermore they were not available from any other source.

The system was a product of the times. In terms of promoting economic development in Latin America it worked. Countries such as Argentina and Chile advanced rapidly. Relative to the highly developed countries they were more advanced then than they are today. Mexico, despite political upheaval, became a leading producer of petroleum. Venezuela became an even more important petroleum producer and could boast that its government had no foreign debt.

Progress was not uniform or equal to what was taking place in the United States and Canada, and in the countries of Western Europe, but it was infinitely greater than it would have been without the aid of foreign capital. The system worked but it had characteristics that would lead to its modification.

The businessman's idea of social responsibility in the 1920's still was relatively primitive, in the developed countries as well as in those that were less developed. The large foreign companies were helpful to the Latin Americans but not as helpful as they could have been. They were disciplined, powerful organizations out to make a profit. Many governments felt small by comparison with them and fearful of the influences they could bring to bear upon them.

I served as Vice-Consul in Tampico, Mexico, during the oil boom of the early 1920's and had an opportunity to observe the attitudes and some of the actions of the large foreign oil companies, most of them American, that were responsible for the boom. Some companies seemed to go out of their way to antagonize Mexicans. At times they gave the impression that they considered themselves above Mexican law. Of course working in Mexico was not easy for foreigners, as it was not easy for Mexicans. The Mexican revolution had uprooted old institutions, and new ones had not yet been firmly established. The government could not count on the loyalty or the honesty of all persons who represented it. It was not easy for the companies to do business in those circumstances. Nevertheless they could have done better than they did, and when the Mexican government later expropriated the companies' properties, it had the support of public opinion in the country and in the rest of Latin America as well.

The large American fruit companies in Central America had little better success in protecting the reputation of American capital in Latin America. I served as Consul at Puerto Castilla, a tiny enclave in the Honduran jungle which was headquarters for one of the fruit companies and loading point for the bananas it produced. The fruit company paid a tax on every stem of bananas exported. The proceeds of the tax were an important source of revenue to the Honduran government and a tempting prize for Honduran political groups.

There was more than one American fruit company in Honduras. Each company tried to influence the Honduran government in its favor, and Honduran politicians played off one company against another with immoderate delight. Opposition groups sought fruit company support by promising more favorable treatment once they were in power, and sometimes they got support. Whether the fruit companies could have stayed clear of politics if they had tried harder is questionable. Possibly they could not have. In any event the fact that they were involved in politics was resented by Hondurans.

No less resented were the companies' labor practices. The fruit company furnished housing for its workers and gave them excellent medical care, the first medical care many of them had ever had. Wages, too, were good according to Honduran standards, but they provided little more than subsistence for workers and families. Nearly all technical and clerical employees of the company were brought down from the United States. Little if any thought appears to have been given to training Hondurans for jobs. With very few exceptions, the only Hondurans employed at good salaries were political fixers. Those persons conducted relations with the local authorities whom the Americans seldom got to know. Our compatriots felt little identity with the people of the country where they were earning their living.

American companies were not the only ones whose practices offended the Latin Americans, and in many areas they were not the principal offenders. Not all the oil companies were American, and not all the companies that offended were oil companies or fruit companies. Argentines (and one British ambassador as well) tell of the arrogance displayed by the directors of the British-owned railroads during their occasional visits to the country, which as described differed from visits of royalty chiefly in the scant attention the directors paid to the officials and people of Argentina, who were made to feel like true colonials.

Nor did Latin Americans behave any better, or were they any more popular when the shoe was on the other foot. In Paraguay I found that the "exploiters" were not the Americans or the British but Paraguay's next door neighbors, the Argentines, the same Argentines who so keenly resented British dominance of the railroad industry in their country.

Our government's role in development, in the twenties, was to extend "protection" to American private interests. Often it seemed that the American interest in a country was little more than the sum of American private interests in that country. A very large part of a diplomat's or a consul's time was taken up in "protecting" those private interests. The Legal Adviser's office at the State Department resembled a huge law firm whose clients were principally Americans doing business abroad. We even used our military power to protect American private interests, and other foreign interests as well. When there was revolution in my consular district in Honduras I could call an American warship to protect foreign interests, and I did so more than once. I could also dispose the landing of bluejackets and marines. Furthermore I could do those things without consulting Washington.

The practices of American private interests and of the United States government inevitably led to the charge of "economic imperialism," and the charge continued to be made years after most of the "imperialists" had passed away and the practices that had given rise to the charge had been abandoned.

The system I was able to observe was a product of the times but times were changing. The early 1930's were difficult years. Economic depression spread over the earth. Latin America as well as other areas felt the pinch, and Latin American governments looked more and more to the rich foreign companies operating in their territory to help relieve their burdens and the burdens of their people. They were quite justified in doing that. Unfortunately, however, the reaction of many governments followed the pendulum rule and went so far, in terms of restrictions and interferences, as to constitute a real obstacle to the further economic development of the Latin American countries.

I do not mean to imply that controls were imposed only on foreign capital. A growing tendency of Latin American governments to play a more direct role in the development process, and later, wartime scarcities, encouraged controls of all kinds. However, early abuses by foreigners contributed importantly to the multiplication of controls and interferences and justified them in the minds of Latin Americans when they were applied principally to foreign companies, many of which, with all their failings, were making contributions which were important and even essential to the economic development of the countries concerned and that, in practice, no one else could make.

President Franklin Roosevelt's Good Neighbor Policy brought about a great change in our government's attitude toward private American interests in Latin America. The new policy said, in effect, that since we had no way of holding American companies accountable for their acts in a foreign country we would leave the government of the country free to perform that sovereign function. We gave up none of our rights under international law, but we chose to exercise those rights with greater consideration of the rights of other countries.

Our government's new attitude helped to bring about a sharp improvement in the performance of American companies in Latin America. The State Department reached agreement with the Mexican government concerning payment for the expropriated oil properties without having been able first to obtain the consent of the companies, and the companies later accepted the agreement. When the government of Venezuela demanded a larger share of the earnings of the foreign oil companies, the department exerted pressure on the American companies to reach an agreement with the government, and they did.

Eduardo Santos, then President of Colombia, described the new situation accurately when he noted that during an earlier period it had been the American companies that had threatened to take their case against the Colombian government to Washington. Now it was the Colombian government that threatened to appeal to Washington against the companies.

I recall the occasion when our change of policy with respect to American investments abroad was brought strikingly to my attention. It was the year 1933 and I was serving in the State Department. An American firm was in trouble with the Dominican government and was trying to induce the department to take up the cudgel in its behalf. However the department declined to intervene. The company looked around for someone who might bring pressure to bear on the department and found a likely helper in the person of a well-known member of the Democratic National Committee. The national committeeman called on Secretary Hull and explained his business. The secretary listened gravely. Then he looked at the department's organizational chart and saw that I was handling Dominican affairs. He referred the committeeman to me.

The committeeman came into my office, which I shared with three colleagues as junior as myself, and stated his case. I was quite familiar with the problem. I told him the State Department could not intervene and explained why. He picked up his hat and walked out, and we never heard from him again with reference to the case, nor did the company try to bring further pressure to bear on us. Cordell Hull, in his austere way, had indicated, unmistakably, that politics was not going to influence decisions in such matters, and that the Department of State was as much concerned with the rights of foreign countries as it was with the rights of American investors.

American companies were quick to perceive that times had changed. I do not hesitate to say, on the basis of my own observation, that today they have the most enlightened policies and practices of all the companies operating in Latin America, including companies operated by nationals of the countries. It would have taken a brave and far-seeing man to predict, thirty or forty years ago, when the fruit companies were being accused of running Central America, that one day the government of a Central American country would approach the government of the United States and plead for financial help to an American fruit company to permit it to expand its operations in that country, but this has occurred.

The government of that Central American country has learned that cooperation between government and foreign private investment can advance the legitimate interests of each, and that in the absence of such cooperation the interests of both may suffer. Unfortunately, not all Latin American governments have learned that lesson sufficiently well.

13. The Guilt Complex

VICE-PRESIDENT NIXON HAD a kind of ambivalence toward the attacks on him in South America. On the one hand he placed blame for them directly on the international Communists. "When I asked for questions at the University [of Buenos Aires]," he said, "Gregorio Selser, a well-known Communist newspaper writer who was thirty-four years old, shouted down other students and stood up to ask a question. His question was a twenty-minute tirade, a good part of which he read from a prepared text, straight out of the Communist line on every international controversy. I recognized him as the leader of the group which had handed out anti-American leaflets outside the University."[1] Mr. Nixon recalled also that the Communists had distributed leaflets in Lima calling on Peruvians to prevent him from speaking at San Marcos University. He identified those who attacked him in Lima and Caracas as Communists and Communist-led, and he gave the Communists principal credit for all the troubles that beset him in South America.

At the same time he took the view that the United States government as well must be in the wrong. He seemed to suggest that what had happened to him was less a Nixon failure in Latin America than a failure of the United States. Soon after his return from Caracas, he made basic recommendations to President Eisenhower concerning ways to remedy what he considered to be our government's deficiencies in that area. "American government personnel abroad [presumably including those who had warned him to abandon his student-baiting plans] must do a more effective job of reaching the opinion-makers of Latin America," he said. "Students, teachers, newspaper editors, reporters, labor leaders—these are the people who are exerting massive influence in the Latin American countries, and we must find a way to get our

1. Richard M. Nixon, *Six Crises*, (New York, 1962), p. 203.

story across to them more adequately."[2] More adequately than he had been able to do, he may have meant, although he was careful not to say so. With rare courage, considering what he had just been through, Mr. Nixon continued, "Person-to-person contact is the most effective way to accomplish this."[3]

Mr. Nixon regarded "what happened in Caracas and Lima as a warning that we could no longer get by with fancy words and little action in dealing with the problems of our neighbors to the South."[4] With that statement he tossed aside the Export-Import Bank, Point IV, the Development Loan Fund, our participation in the World Bank and United Nations aid programs, and other contributions the United States government was making to development in Latin America.

Mr. Nixon, in his memorandum, went on to make recommendations concerning the attitudes we should take toward democracy, toward dictators, toward the military forces, and toward other phenomena in Latin America. If his recommendations today sound like a collection of meaningless platitudes, they do not differ greatly in that respect from many other reports of high officials of our government who have gained their background on Latin America during brief official visits to the area.

Mr. Nixon, in placing a degree of guilt upon the government of the United States and particularly on its representatives abroad, may have been bothered principally by his own feeling of guilt. He may, consciously or subconsciously, have been trying to remove a part of the blame for the incidents from his own shoulders and place it on the more anonymous shoulders of those who bear the day-to-day burden of working with the Latin Americans. Whatever his reasons he helped to set a style, and until recently the style had changed very little.

The Alliance for Progress produced a great wave of breast-beating on the part of high officials of the Kennedy administration. The State Department's Legal Advisor, the Honorable Abram Chayes, in an emotional speech in San Antonio before the State Junior Bar of Texas, on July 5, 1962, said,

There is a way to measure the dimensions of our recent neglect. Of the $90.5 billion worth of U.S. financial assistance abroad since

2. *Ibid.*, p. 246.
3. *Ibid.*
4. *Ibid.*

the war, Latin America, close to us geographically and historically and of obvious strategic importance, has had only $5 billion.

We can adduce reasons for this decade and a half of neglect. But history does not accept excuses. In our own hemisphere, as elsewhere, slums, poverty, sickness, ignorance, exploited peasants and indifferent rulers are the breeding ground of revolution, a revolution all too vulnerable to capture by the adversaries of freedom.

By September 1960, when the Act of Bogotá finally took the first step toward redressing the balance, the danger had come to reality. Castro was in the saddle in Cuba. His agents and imitators found willing ears throughout the hemisphere. The secure southern flank which we had taken for granted was beginning to seeth and buckle. It was, as Dr. José Figueres, former President of Costa Rica, said, "one minute to midnight."

The Honorable Mr. Chayes doubtless is distinguished as well as Honorable, but on July 5, 1962, he was far from being an authority on Latin America or on our aid efforts in that area. Nor was his logic impressive. The figures of $90.5 billion and $5 billion were meaningless by themselves. If by spending $90.5 billion dollars the United States helped to save the free world from anarchy and disintegration and from domination by communism, it was money well spent, from the standpoint of Latin American as well as United States interest. If spending twice that amount had been needed to achieve our objectives, then the larger amount also would have been well spent. On the other hand, if spending $5 billion to help Latin America did little good, it may have been money poorly spent, from any standpoint.

The device of comparing sums spent in different places or for different purposes in an effort to obtain increases in the lower sum is a familiar one. It is used almost yearly to justify increased appropriations for the United States Information Agency. The argument, with which Congressional Committees now are quite familiar, is that appropriations for USIA should be increased because the cost of running USIA for a year is less than the cost of building a single aircraft carrier. A few years ago the comparison used to be with a battleship, which costs less to build than an aircraft carrier. That represents progress, so far as sums involved are concerned. But the sophistry is the same.

M. Jean Daniel, a French writer, had a long talk with President Kennedy on October 24, 1963. Cuba was one of the principal topics of the conversation. M. Daniel quotes Mr. Kennedy as saying

I believe that there is no country in the world, including all the African regions, including any and all the countries under colonial domination, where economic colonization, humiliation and exploitation were worse than in Cuba, in part owing to my country's policies during the Batista regime. I believe that we created, built and manufactured the Castro movement out of whole cloth and without realizing it. I believe that the accumulation of these mistakes has jeopardized all of Latin America. The great aim of the Alliance for Progress is to reverse this unfortunate policy. This is one of the most, if not the most, important problems in American foreign policy. I can assure you that I have understood the Cubans. I approved the proclamation which Fidel Castro made in the Sierra Maestra, when he justifiably called for justice and especially yearned to rid Cuba of corruption. I will go even further: to some extent it is as though Batista was the incarnation of a number of sins on the part of the United States. Now we shall have to pay for those sins.[5]

President Kennedy died before M. Daniel's report was published, and he therefore had no opportunity to comment on it. Nevertheless the views attributed to him resemble those of many persons in his administration. Furthermore it would have been surprising if his own feeling of guilt concerning Cuba had not increased following the Bay of Pigs operation, and if he had not been willing, as Mr. Nixon had been before him, to share a portion of that guilt with other Americans in government.

Breast-beating can be a helpful exercise. It assuages feelings of guilt, relieves tensions, and makes one feel better about himself if not about his predecessors. It may also open the door to more helpful attitudes. But guilt is not usually one-sided. When breast-beating is unilateral, it may also create new problems.

Breast-beating by American officials was aimed largely at arousing support in the United States for our program of aid to Latin America. Some of it of course also was aimed at attracting the votes of Mexican-Americans, Cuban-Americans, and other minority groups. But it was heard not only in the United States but also in Latin America, where it made headlines in the press. The idea that the United States might be responsible for Latin

5. M. Jean Daniel, "Unofficial Envoy: An Historic Report from Two Capitals," *New Republic,* December 14, 1963, p. 15.

America's failures was not new. Many Latin American "intellectuals" and a few Latin American political leaders had taken that view for years. It was some of the latter who had sold it to the Eisenhower and Kennedy administrations. But the Latin American people, who perhaps know their leaders better than politicians in Washington know them, had never fully accepted the idea.

On the other hand, when American leaders themselves placed the finger of blame on the United States it occurred to many persons in Latin America that there must be something to it. Perhaps the rioters in Lima and Caracas did have just grievances. Forgotten for the moment, or submerged, were Latin America's own failures, it's own inadequacies. These existed, no one doubted, but they did not make headlines as United States' failures did and it was easy to put them aside.

Dr. Alberto Lleras Camargo, former President of Colombia and one of Latin America's most respected statesmen, said in August 1963,

> Unfortunately there are still governments, peoples, landlords, capitalists, revolutionaries of the extreme right, Castro agents, inviting the peoples of Latin America to wait and see what the United States is going to do to rescue them from their poverty. That is the most fallacious distortion of the Alliance, and surely the most dangerous, because it fits in with the laziness of governments and the desire always to have a whipping boy for all the defects, vices and errors of any administration. And the United States is the biggest and best whipping boy since the time of the Greeks.[6]

To the degree that the United States made itself a whipping boy for Latin America's failures, the possibility that Latin Americans would improve their own performance was of course diminished. This was less than a happy circumstance because without improved performance by Latin Americans, the Alliance for Progress could not succeed.

6. "Estabilidad y fijeza," *Vision*, August 9, 1963, p. 21.

14. Demagogy and Nationalism

THE PRINCIPAL OBSTACLE to democracy and to progress in Latin America is not communism, although the Communists do all they can to prevent progress, nor oligarchs, although many an oligarch finds it difficult to see beyond the confines of his own latifundio. The principal obstacle to progress is demagogy, which usually masquerades as the purest kind of democracy.

The Communists are master demagogues of course. And even oligarchs are not above resorting to demagogy in order to protect their economic privileges and to gain or retain political power. President Goulart, a millionaire landowner, carried Brazil a long way toward chaos or communism with his demagogic policies. Plagued by poverty and, all too often, by ignorance, Latin Americans tend to be ready victims of demagogy. They seek quick, easy solutions to their vexing problems, and that is what the demagogue offers them. The political leader who stresses blood, sweat, and tears does not usually go far in Latin America. Instead of emphasizing unremitting and cooperative effort by citizens, the political leader offers himself and the power of the State as their saviors.

We in the United States are no strangers to demagogy. Every four years we are privileged to watch, on our television sets, the national conventions of the two major political parties and much of the campaign for the presidency. We see otherwise honorable men attack the opposition party and the opposition candidate with innuendo, exaggeration, and sometimes with plain falsehood. It is hard to beat our politicians, or many of them at least, in the field of demagogy. I would put them up against the best. Happily for us and for our democratic system, however, the use of demagogy, so far at least, has diminished after the excitement and fervor of elections have subsided, and people in both parties have settled down to face reality and to make the democratic system work.

But in Latin America, in too many cases, the sort of demagogy that characterizes our electoral campaigns never subsides. Furthermore, in the atmosphere of nationalism that usually exists, it is frequently the foreigner who is the target. Demagogy feeds on nationalism, and all Latin American countries are highly nationalistic. If patriotism is sometimes the last refuge of scoundrels, as we say in our country, then nationalism, in Latin America, is frequently a substitute for patriotism.

The United States has power unequaled by that of any other nation in the free world. And yet its foreign policy stresses the interdependence of nations. Its experience in exercising responsibility, or trying to exercise it, has demonstrated the degree to which even the most powerful nation depends on other nations—for resources it does not possess, for markets it requires, for support and cooperation in an increasing number of fields.

In contrast Latin Americans, who tend to rate low in the power scale, are obsessed with the idea of independence. This doubtless is a reaction to fear. One clings most tightly to what one fears to lose. The growing economic, political, and military gap between Latin America and the more developed nations emphasizes Latin America's weakness, her dependence, and causes Latin Americans to feel exposed and left behind.

Nationalism is a natural phenomenon in Latin America, and in many ways a helpful one. It has been a kind of bulwark against communism. A leading nationalist in a large South American country, a man with an excellent education who has taught in one of our leading universities, told me that he would not be a nationalist if he knew any other device for holding his country together, but he knew no other. Divided by racial origins, by social stratification, by economic interest and by excessive regionalism and individualism, his people could become a nation, he thought, only if they were held together by nationalism.

If nationalism in Latin America is a tie it also is an escape valve. It relieves frustration. It should not be confused with anti-Americanism, although it may take an anti-American turn. Even then it is rarely directed against Americans as persons. I have stood in the middle of a Latin American crowd more than once and listened to orators attack the United States in violent language, while persons around me who knew who I was smiled at me reassuringly.

Persons who know Latin America were quick to recognize that the mob that insulted Mr. Nixon in Lima was not Latin American or Peruvian, although it was made up of Peruvians. It had all the earmarks of having been assembled by international Communists. Foreign Service officers who followed Mr. Nixon's electioneering and student-baiting with justified concern were surprised that no mob had attacked the vice-president before he reached Lima.

Justified or not, impersonal or not, Latin American nationalism is a ready-made excuse for official irresponsibility and failure, and in that sense it is a serious impediment to progress. Nationalism always is close to the surface of Latin American politics. Castro's action in seizing foreign-owned properties without compensation was a blow to the owners of those properties, but it was a much more serious blow to the other American republics. With our tendency to lump all Latin American countries together, and with our government and press warning that Castroism might spread beyond Cuba, new foreign private capital decided, in general, to stay out of Latin America until the new situation could be evaluated. Latin American political leaders, if they had been wiser, might have hastened to repudiate Castro's action, but few did. Many got a degree of satisfaction out of it. Their countries paid for that satisfaction and will continue to pay for it.

The threat of expropriation is never absent in Latin America. When the United States government openly espoused agrarian reform in Chile the large landowners in the Chilean Congress proposed that the government expropriate the American-owned copper mines in Chile. They suggested, furthermore, that since the United States government had such a liberal attitude toward the things it considered Chileans should do in their own country, it probably would be willing to lend the Chilean government the funds it needed to compensate the American owners.

Latin Americans, time and time again, have complained about foreign mining companies that have more than recovered their original investment but still continue to remit profits abroad while they deplete a mineral resource that is irreplaceable. "What these foreign companies do," say the nationalists, "is to drain the country of its foreign exchange and then leave it nothing but a hole in the ground." The charge might not stand up under analysis, but it is a favorite topic for demagogy and in Latin America's nationalistic ambience it sounds quite plausible.

The issue usually is falsely presented of course. Domestic capital is just as capable of leaving holes in the ground as foreign capital is. But it is likely to pay a much smaller tax than the foreigner does. And it is capable of remitting abroad a higher percentage of its earnings than the foreigner remits. The flight of Latin American capital abroad is a problem that neither the Alliance for Progress nor the earnest pleadings of Latin American governments have been able to make much of an impression on.

When I was Ambassador to Chile, the government of that country was taxing the American-owned copper mining companies at a rate that reached 83 percent of earnings in some cases (Chilean companies paid at a lower rate because they were Chilean). The 83 percent represented dollars that went not abroad but directly into the Chilean government's treasury. A tax rate of 83 percent is close to being confiscatory, and it was later reduced to a possible 52½ percent. In practice, however, it has continued to be higher than sixty percent. The tax collected from the American copper companies is the Chilean government's principal source of foreign exchange and the guarantee of its solvency. The companies' profit from their operations is modest compared with the profit the Chilean government continues to earn in the form of taxes collected. Moreover, the government earns its profit without having had to invest a penny in the industry or to assume any of the exceptional risks that are inseparable from mining.

Despite this favorable situation, the Chilean government, making liberal use of the threat of expropriation, has induced the Board of Directors of the Anaconda Company to recommend that the company sell its two largest mines in Chile to the government. The government already is 51 percent owner of the country's third major copper mine, formerly the property of the Kennecott Copper Company.

Nationalism impelled the Illia government in Argentina to cancel the drilling contracts that an earlier administration had entered into with American petroleum companies, despite the circumstance that the companies had made it possible for Argentina to become self-sufficient in petroleum products. The contracts were renegotiated by a later government, but meanwhile Argentina's economy had lost uncounted millions of dollars it could not afford to lose.

Late in 1968 a Peruvian military junta seized properties of the International Petroleum Company, an American-owned company, valued at some $200 million. The Belaunde government, which the junta overthrew, had just reached an agreement with the American-owned company settling a long-standing dispute that had become a political football in Peru. The junta's action was less an example of Peruvian militarism than of Peruvian nationalism. Unless prompt and adequate compensation to the owners of the properties is offered by the Peruvian government, American aid, as well as the sugar quota subsidy Peru is receiving from the United States, probably will be canceled under the provisions of the Hickenlooper amendment to our aid legislation. In that event, not only will much of the benefit that may have resulted from the more than $600 million of economic aid already extended to Peru be lost, but relations between the two countries will be seriously affected.

Demagogy and nationalism impair the ambience for foreign investment. They also impair the ambience for foreign aid.

15. Government as Entrepreneur

PRIVATE CAPITAL, as we have seen, was downgraded in the Act of Bogotá and the Alliance for Progress, although it had been responsible for most material progress in Latin America in the past. Nor is there often any real discussion of its role among the governments of the American republics. Investment, to the extent that it is discussed at inter-American meetings, means principally investment by government or investment in which government has a principal role, because those are the kinds of investments the Latin Americans are willing to discuss. Inter-American meetings are meetings of government representatives, and Latin American governments are committed to enlarging their role in the economic field. Or to phrase it differently, politicians and bureaucrats in Latin America are committed to enlarging the role of politicians and bureaucrats in the economic field.

Furthermore, since our government acts on the premise that inter-American meetings must end in agreement, the agreements we have subscribed to have provided for an ever greater role for public investment. In the case of the Alliance for Progress, of course, its American authors as well as those Latin Americans who influenced them had their own predilections for increases in public investment.

Nevertheless Professor Gordon, in his book on the Alliance, considered it prudent to warn Latin American governments concerning the possible disadvantages of relying excessively on state-owned enterprise.

Obviously each nation must make its own decisions as to the range of economic operations it wishes to be managed directly by the government. It should be noted, however, that it is not easy to organize efficient public administration even for the minimum functions which any modern government undertakes. On the social side, there is the huge task of modernizing the educational system, including the provision of universal primary education, technical and vocational secondary education, and higher education redesigned to meet the needs for specialized manpower for rapid progress. Systems of public health, social security, and agricultural extension services are additional major governmental tasks whose successful organization is essential to rapid modernization. On the economic side, there are the basic networks of transportation, communications, and supply of power and water, in all of which government operation and government financing necessarily play a large part.

How far a nation wishes to go beyond this in operating certain basic industries depends partly on the availability of private resources for these purposes and partly on political considerations which each community must evaluate for itself.

From the point of view of efficient development, the important requirement is that such public enterprises be well operated—technically, administratively, and economically. And it would be simply blindness not to recognize that there are certain built-in obstacles, which are not easy to overcome. There is the problem of avoiding political criteria in the selection of personnel. There is the problem of avoiding excessive centralization of what are essentially business-type decisions. And there is the problem of applying objective accounting standards to costs and expenditures to avoid hidden subsidies really made at the expense of the people themselves.

In nations which have a long tradition of highly efficient public administration, such as England, Switzerland, and Germany, these obstacles are largely overcome by organizing government enterprises on a true business basis, completely insulated from politics. In other countries, the experiences generally have been less successful. It is significant that Socialist political parties in the free countries of Western Europe have in recent years tended to abandon state operation of industry as a political goal, finding that private operations within a framework of governmental regulation which encourages competition and ensures fair treatment of labor and consumers are better guarantors of high productivity and of social justice than are the outmoded theories of state socialization. And as to agriculture, surely even the more doctrinaire Communists must be harboring doubts about collective and communal farms which provide neither adequate production nor even political satisfaction for the peasants.[1]

It is ironic that, as Professor Gordon delicately suggests, many

---

1. Lincoln Gordon, *A New Deal for Latin America; The Alliance for Progress*, (Cambridge, Mass., 1963), p. 84.

Latin American governments are lagging behind the Socialist governments of Europe in recognizing the value of private capital's contribution to development, and that in some countries the lag is becoming greater under the Alliance for Progress.

Consider the case of Argentina, a country of vast natural wealth, which a few years ago was moving forward at about the same rate Haiti was. When Juan Domingo Peron, an ardent nationalist, became President of Argentina in 1946, he proceeded to "Argentinize" the American-owned telephone system in Buenos Aires and the British-owned railroads in the country. Unlike latter-day nationalists in other countries, Peron paid for those enterprises and paid well for them, much to the gratification of their former owners who were happy to be rid of them. The Argentine nation paid even more dearly.

Getting a telephone put in your home in Buenos Aires may be a labor of months, and then it doesn't work a good deal of the time. The railroads have been featherbedded and politicized beyond bankruptcy. Service has deteriorated as costs have risen. Petroleum is produced in Argentina by a government-owned "monopoly." Strangely enough Peron, during the final years of his presidency, and doubtless because he felt he had no alternative, flew in the face of his own and Argentine nationalism when he negotiated a contract with an American company to come in and help produce more petroleum. The contract was never carried out. It was one of the causes of Peron's fall from power.

Ousting Peron did nothing to lessen Argentina's burden of paying for imports of petroleum which the country was capable of producing with help from the outside. When Arturo Frondizi became president in May of 1958, those imports were costing some $300 million a year, which roughly approximated the deficit in the country's international balance of payments. The deficit had helped to exhaust Argentina's foreign exchange reserves while the country's external debt mounted and its economy was deprived not only of consumer goods that Argentines customarily purchased abroad but also of production goods urgently needed to maintain Argentina's industrial plant. Frondizi had been a leader in the movement to keep the foreign oil companies out of Argentina. Nevertheless one of the early acts of his government was to enter into contracts with various foreign companies with the purpose of making Argentina self-sufficient in petroleum. That purpose was substantially accomplished.

President Frondizi, like President Peron, was forced out of office and the elected government that followed proceeded promptly to annul the petroleum contracts as "unconstitutional" and contrary to Argentina's interest. That government too was overthrown. The latest government to come to power has negotiated new contracts with the American companies. The dreary cycle continues.

The Argentine government owns and operates not only telephone companies, railroads, and a petroleum "monopoly," but also steel mills, power companies, and a very large number of industrial plants. A major portion of the government's enormous budgetary deficit is accounted for by the losses of these state-owned enterprises. But the tragic recital does not end there. Argentina's budgetary deficit has been a cause of mounting inflation with its sequel of rising living costs, labor troubles, political unrest, and lessened confidence in Argentina as a place for investment.

There are few, if any Latin American countries where statism has not taken hold. The following table shows the percentage of public ownership of the ten largest enterprises in each of the countries listed:

Argentina	84.5
Brazil	78.1
Chile (excluding copper and nitrate exporters)	75.9
Colombia (excluding petroleum companies)	69.4
Mexico	100
Venezuela (excluding petroleum companies)	87.7[2]

Professor Gordon, in his role as Assistant Secretary of State and United States Coordinator for the Alliance for Progress, had this to say during a Congressional Hearing on the Alliance when he was asked to comment on the extent of new private United States investment in Latin America:

Exact statistics on the extent of private U.S. investment are difficult to obtain. We do know that approximately $18 million of new foreign investment took place in Mexico during 1966 and we

2. Frank Brandenburg, *The Development of Latin American Private Enterprise,* (Washington, D. C., 1964), p. 66.

assume that most of this investment was from the United States. Over the past 5 years a number of studies have indicated that an average of $250 million per year of new foreign investment has entered Latin America as a whole. This figure, however, is the net input; that is, the difference between capital repatriated and new capital entering.

There does not seem to be any long-term trend toward increased investment of any importance taking place with the exception of Mexico. However, individual countries or areas do enjoy periods of improved investment climate. For example the Central American Common Market area is now, and has been for a number of years, enjoying increased attention by increasing numbers of U.S. firms. Brazil, after its low point of 1965, is beginning again to attract active interest on the part of a large number of U.S. and other foreign companies. Argentina, during the Illia regime of 1963–66, attracted very little new foreign investment. However, the Ongania government which took power in June 1966 is now in the process of creating improved investment conditions and, again, foreign firms are beginning to look seriously at Argentina. Chile has a number of large projects underway, but in general the investment community is circumspect in view of Chile's strong orientation toward state-dominated industries. Peru currently is enjoying a better than average flow of new foreign capital.[3]

A brief analysis of this testimony sheds considerable light not only on the investment climate in Latin America but also on the complexities and contradictions of our program of aid to Latin America in the context of our total diplomacy in that area.

Brazil's "low point" of 1965 reflected the policies of an elected government. It required military intervention in the nation's politics to reverse the downward trend. The Illia regime in Argentina which "attracted little foreign investment" was a democratically elected regime. It was the regime that canceled the contracts that the Frondizi government had signed with American petroleum companies. On the other hand the Ongania government, which was "in the process of creating improved investment conditions" in Argentina, is a military government. It deposed the Illia regime and renegotiated the petroleum contracts with the American companies.

While it is true that at the time Secretary Gordon testified

---

3. U.S., Congress, House, Subcommittee of the Committee on Appropriations, *Hearing on Foreign Operations and Related Agencies: Economic Assistance,* 90th Cong., 1st sess., 1968, p. 1511, pt. 2.

Peru was "enjoying a better than average flow of private capital" it is doubtful, in the light of the Peruvian government's seizure of the International Petroleum Company's properties, that this will continue to be the case.

Secretary Gordon's comment that "the investment community is circumspect in view of Chile's strong orientation toward state-dominated industries" may have been an understatement. The Chilean government today exercises a monopoly or has a majority ownership in petroleum production and refining, steel production, electric power, railroads, commercial aviation, and sales of nitrate. It also owns and operates many other industries and businesses and, as we have seen, is buying into the copper mining industry as a partner of the large American companies. Chile, together with Brazil and Colombia, has been a favored recipient of United States aid.

Some officials in the State Department have been playing an interesting game. It involves placing bets on which country will make greater progress in the years to come, military-dominated Argentina, which is receiving very little aid from our government, or democratic Chile, which is receiving a great deal of United States aid. There are takers on both sides.

16. Aid and the Military

ONE OF THE OBJECTIVES of the Marshall Plan was to help place the nations of Western Europe in a position to defray the costs of their own defense. The threat of Communist imperialism was clear and imminent, and it was equally clear that Western Europe should play its appropriate role in meeting it.

But the problem facing the Alliance for Progress in the military field was totally different. It was how to induce most of the Latin American countries to reduce their expenditures for armaments. Given the important political role the military play in Latin America this was a difficult objective to achieve and in practice little or no progress has been made in achieving it.

The planners who met at Harvard University were well aware that the burden of armaments was retarding development in most Latin American countries. "We hope the Latin American people will recognize," they said, "that the present level of expenditure on military establishments is incompatible with the limited financial resources available. This is particularly true if the lateness of the hour is kept in mind and if we are to act in time to meet the urgent and huge social and economic imperatives which confront the Alliance. In principle there must be agreement by the Latin American nations to reduce their military outlay to that needed for internal security."

Following this cue President Kennedy, in his White House address to the Latin American diplomats, made reduction of military expenditures one of his major points. "We [the United States] reaffirm our pledge to come to the defense of any American nation whose independence is endangered," he said. "As confidence in the collective security system of the OAS spreads, it will be possible to devote to constructive use a major share of those resources now spent on the instruments of war. Even now, as the Government of Chile has said, the time has come to take the first steps toward sensible limitations of arms."

However the Charter of Punta del Este is silent on the question of arms limitation. Perhaps in the light of the Castro threat, and the degree to which the United States government was stressing it, there was little reason to expect that military expenditures in Latin America would soon be reduced or limited. Nor did Latin America's pre-Castro history offer much hope in that field.

President Jorge Alessandri of Chile, it is true, had made a courageous proposal that expenditures for armaments be limited but Chile is one of the more fortunate countries where military intervention in politics has not been a great problem in recent years. And the government of the United States continued, at various times and in various ways, to suggest action along the same line, but neither the Latin American military nor most of the Latin American governments appeared to be listening.

The United States government of course has a military assistance program as well as an economic aid program in Latin America, and naturally there is a relationship between the two. Whether the military program has been helpful to the purposes of the aid program or even to relations with the Latin American countries is open to question. While economic progress in Latin America has been disappointingly slow during the period the programs have been in effect, Latin America, in the field of armaments,has moved from the mid-nineteenth century to the early twentieth century, and in some respects even further.

It is the custom in most Latin American countries to celebrate the national holiday with an elaborate military demonstration. I recall particularly the one that took place in Santiago, Chile's capital city, on September 18, 1955. With the meager armaments they had at the time Chilean soldiers had more time for drilling than many armies have and they were close to being letter perfect on the parade ground. The ski troops in their white uniforms were picturesque and impressive. Army cadets goose-stepped in the best Prussian and Chilean tradition. But the men on horseback were the most impressive of all. There was a large body of cavalry mounted on spirited animals. There also was a mounted band. The demonstration reached its climax when the horse-drawn artillery thundered past the reviewing stand at a breathtaking gallop.

It happened that I had as my guest at the demonstration that year a United States congressman from a southern state. He was fascinated by what he saw—especially by the horse-drawn artillery. "Why there hasn't been anything like this since the Civil War!" he said to me admiringly. That doubtless was true so far as the United States was concerned, but it was far from being true in Chile. Demonstrations of the kind he had witnessed were traditional in that country, and in other Latin American countries as well. Nevertheless changes were going on in Latin America, and the United States military assistance program was partly responsible for them.

Our present program was started at the time of the Korean War when we were wooing the Latin American governments and the Latin American military in the hope that they might send troops to Korea. Only Colombia did, and Colombia's decision was probably not related to the program. However the program, in characteristic fashion, developed a momentum of its own, which has continued until today.

Even in 1955 the Chilean army was the proud possessor of a collection of United States army tanks sent down under our assistance program. The tanks did not appear in the demonstration that the congressman and I witnessed. In fact many Chileans were not aware that they existed. But the Chilean army was. When student disorders broke out in Santiago, a Chilean army general said to me with some emotion, "I could put a stop to this sort of thing in five minutes if they would let me bring some of those tanks down from Antofagasta." Antofagasta is a city in Chile's Atacama desert. During a visit to the city I found an opportunity to drive out several miles to inspect the tanks and to observe the pride the Chilean army had in them. They were medium tanks but they looked like huge mastodons in their desert lair. They were obsolete according to American standards, but in Chilean eyes they were the latest things. They were nearly immobilized because few bridges in the area were strong enough to support them. And they consumed so much fuel that the Chilean army could afford to run their engines only a few minutes a week. But they were cared for with love and they shone as no army tank in the United States has ever shone.

When the United States government sent tanks to Chile it considered that the proper role of the Latin American military was to contribute to continental defense. But it changed that view after Castro showed his colors. President Kennedy's pledge that the United States would "come to the defense of any American nation whose independence is endangered" was not new. It had become a basic tenet in our military strategy. In today's world of massive and deadly armaments only the United States is capable of defending Latin America against assault from beyond the continent. A Latin American country can engage in war today only against its next door neighbor, and even that kind of war would not be permitted to go on long, unless the peace-keeping arrangements of the Organization of American States are mere scraps of paper that is. If it should develop that they are no more than that, then our whole military posture vis-à-vis the rest of the continent would have to be reviewed and possibly revised.

Our strategists consider that the mission of Latin America's military today should be internal security. What Latin American countries need, it is now believed, are not armies and navies prepared to reenact a miniature World War I or World War II, but police forces capable of resisting internal subversion and maintaining law and order throughout the area. Armaments above that level of activity serve principally to bolster the pride and the vanity of the military and to enhance national "prestige." But acquiring sophisticated armaments is like eating peanuts. Once you start it is hard to stop. The Latin American military show no signs of wanting to stop. And what the military in one country acquire the military next door clamor for, too.

Brazil decided, in the late fifties, that it wanted an aircraft carrier. It asked the United States if it had one it could spare but the United States said it had none. However Great Britain had one that it was quite ready to exchange for pounds sterling, and Brazil bought it. For several years the carrier was out of service in Brazil because it had not been decided whether the planes to be flown from its decks should be navy planes or air force planes.

When Brazil acquired a carrier it was in the cards that the Argentine navy would want one too. Today Argentina as well as Brazil has a carrier. The most important role these carriers probably will play will be that of "influencing" political developments within the two countries. And of course the Brazilian and Argentine armies and air forces will seek and probably find ways to offset the navy's influence by obtaining additional costly armaments of their own.

Many of the Latin American military are no longer interested in "obsolete" armaments. They want the best that are available and they are prepared to pay full price for them—in Europe if the United States will not make them available. In fact Latin America's insistence on acquiring more sophisticated and more expensive armaments has assumed grotesque proportions in the light of the basic poverty of the Latin Americans and their modest defense needs.

Latin American governments are quite ready to quote "statistics" demonstrating that expenditures on armaments are low compared with expenditures of many other countries, and State Department and AID officials have been known to quote those statistics approvingly in their justifications of both economic and military aid. But comparisons with other countries may be a form of sophistry, like saying that USIA costs less than an aircraft carrier. The point is not whether Latin American countries are spending less of their GNP on armaments than Malawi or Mali, for example. The point is that Latin America is spending much more on armaments than it needs to spend and much more than it can afford. Even from the military viewpoint excessive expenditures for armaments are harmful because they make it more difficult to develop the economic strength without which any country is militarily weak.

Needless armaments create a real problem for Latin America. Money spent on arms cannot be spent for economic development, and therefore development is retarded. The problem is political as well because the military in many countries are in a position to enforce their will on their governments with the aid of weapons they may have received from the government of the United States or that they may have purchased with their nations' scarce foreign exchange.

It has become evident that to an unconscionable degree resources which the United States government, and to a lesser degree other governments and international agencies, have made available to many Latin American countries, have had the result of freeing domestic resources which were then invested in unneeded armaments and that this has been harmful to the Latin American countries.

The United States government does not like this. Neither do many Latin American governments, but given the political power of the military they can do little about it. The Latin American president who tries to limit or reduce military expenditures may find that he has been replaced by a military junta.

However the United States Congress has felt it can do something about it. Appropriations for military assistance, and of course for economic assistance as well, have been steadily reduced. Furthermore, a provision of our aid legislation requires AID, in extending economic assistance, to take into account the percentage of a country's budget that is devoted to military purposes, and the degree to which a country is using its foreign exchange to acquire military equipment. Another provision requires AID to withhold assistance to a country in an amount equivalent to the amount the country may have spent for the purchase of sophisticated weapons systems.

At the time President Belaunde approved a settlement of the Peruvian government's dispute with the International Petroleum Company, United States aid to Peru was being severely curtailed. The United States government, in reducing aid, had in mind not only the Peruvian government's treatment of the company, which it considered was harmful to Peru's economy as well as to the company, but also the circumstance that the Peruvian military had purchased a number of costly jet aircraft in Europe, the acquisition of which was difficult to justify from either the economic or military standpoint.

The Peruvian military group that seized power in 1968 was aware of our government's attitude toward the purchase because it had been conveyed in numerous conversations between the two governments. As we have seen, one of the junta's first acts after seizing power was to cancel the agreement the deposed president had entered into with the American petroleum company and to seize the large property that had been the subject of the agreement. Whether or not the actions of the Peruvian military had in them elements of reprisal against the United States, there is no doubt that by taking a stand on the nature and amount of expenditures a foreign government makes on armaments the United States government is injecting itself directly into the internal politics of the country, and in a manner which is capable of having unfortunate effects on those politics and on relations between the country and the United States.

This of course is one of many side effects that accompany aid and make it a most complex phenomenon. No country likes a foreign government to interfere in its internal affairs. On the other hand the United States government, or at least the United States Congress, is not disposed to help finance wasteful military programs that slow down rather than advance economic development.

Our military not only have helped to train Latin American military forces and furnished them equipment. They also have encouraged and aided them to expand their roles in nonmilitary fields, in what the United States government calls "civic action." "Civic action" is the term the Defense Department has applied to activities, such as road building, bridge construction, and furnishing medical care to persons in thinly populated areas, that the military are capable of engaging in, although the activities do not have primarily military purposes.

Civic action, as it has been pressed upon the Latin Americans, has many objectives. One obviously is to provide services that are helpful to a nation's economy and to the well-being of its citizens. Another is to improve the "image" of the military and of the government vis-à-vis the citizens of a country. Still another purpose, one that is seldom stated and is not shared by most of the Latin American military, is to divert the military from warlike pursuits for which there is little justification and to enlist them in helping to carry out the broader aims of the nation.

Civic action is not new by any means, although the name may be new. The Engineer Corps of the United States Army has had a long and impressive record of civic action. Its support in the Congress, especially among senators and representatives from states that want dams and other public works constructed at Federal expense, is so great that it is sometimes beyond the power of the president of the United States to defy it or alter it.

Civic action is not new in Latin America either, although some of its proponents among our military seem to think it is. In the early 1940's, for example, President Fulgencio Batista, in Cuba, practiced civic action with *élan*. Among other things, General-President Batista made schoolteachers out of army sergeants and put them to work in rural areas. According to Cuban government reports at the time, the program was highly successful; literacy increased substantially. Impartial observers in Cuba had no doubt that President Batista's political popularity also increased as a result of civic action.

Some Latin American military leaders have supported civic action with measured enthusiasm. But few have shown a willingness to support it at the expense of purely military duties or functions. Interest in building bridges or draining swamps has not materially lessened interest in late-model tanks and jet fighter-bombers. Nonmilitary functions have in no sense been considered a substitute for military functions. They have been considered additional to them. Military attention has not been diverted but broadened. And in some cases military influence probably has been broadened too.

There are hundreds of reports in the Pentagon relating the success of United States aided civic action programs in Latin America. Many were written by high ranking officers, following brief visits that were accompanied by generous entertainment by Latin American colleagues. Civic action has had importance in Latin America for many years and it will continue to have importance. But our involvement in civic action is filled with subtleties that may escape officials in the Pentagon or indeed anyone who is little experienced in the ways of Latin America and Latin Americans.

A sample of civic action "in action" was revealed during a Senate Hearing on Defense Department Sponsored Foreign Affairs Research on May 9, 1968. I shall let the record speak for itself.

The Chairman [Senator Fulbright]: Senator Mundt, you raised exactly the question I raised in the beginning. The question is not that some of these activities are not interesting to everybody, but whether or not this is the responsibility of the Defense Department.

There are a great many of these. Another is called Resettlement in Latin America, an Analysis of 35 Cases.

The summary gives an indication of what it is about. I will read a paragraph or two just to indicate it. They call it the concluding synthesis: "From a review of written reports of more than 100 Latin American settlements, 35 settlements were selected for study where the most complete data were available. The 35 cases were systematically compared in order to determine whether any factors were significantly related to the success of resettlement.

"The analysis indicated that physical characteristics of the settlements, namely, the quality of the soils, favorable terrain and accessibility are significantly correlated with success. The resettlements, consisting of parcels over 25 hectares, about 50 acres in size, were most likely to be successful. All settlements with a homogeneous population succeeded, while about one-third of the settlements with heterogeneous composition failed.

"For the convenience of individuals and organizations charged with planning and implementing resettlement programs, pertinent guidelines are presented in capsule form. Resettlement must be viewed as a long range program. Careful preparatory work in planning maximizes success. Long-term financing of the entire enterprise, and a solid credit structure should be well established. Land selection should be based on scientific study of the soils, terrain, health conditions and water supply. The selection of crops should be made on the basis of soils, climate and marketability. Parcel sizes should be based on scientific assessments of soils, terrain, crops and family size. Projections of production, using primitive and modern farming techniques, should be made. The settlements should be located near good transportation. Proximity to population and marketing centers is also desirable. Settlers should be selected through a screening process, although more research is needed in this area. Prior farming experience and adaptability are fairly well established criteria."[1]

Senator Fulbright, obviously perplexed by what he had read, continued,

It is difficult for me to see what interest this is to the Army. These are settlements of agricultural people, I suppose, out of the northeast section of Brazil.

It may be a very worthwhile project, but I find it very difficult to say that we ought to appropriate money to the Defense Department to investigate the soils.

If anybody is going to do research in this area I would think it would be Agriculture or AID.

The Defense Department later furnished the committee the following explanation of the material Senator Fulbright had read at the hearing:

One of the missions of the United States Army is to advise, on their request, the armies of developing nations on their missions within their countries. In many developing nations, the indigenous armies are actively engaged in civic action programs such as resettlement. Generally, the local government desires to resettle people in an area offering greater potential and stability for their future exis-

---

1. U.S., Congress, Senate, Committee on Foreign Relations, *Hearings on Defense Department Sponsored Foreign Affairs Research*, 90th Cong., 2d sess., 9 May 1968, p. 34.

tence. In many cases the indigenous army is given the assignment to carry out the program. If U.S. military officers are to be successful in advising their counterparts on such matters, then it is important to estimate the effectiveness of the planned programs. To illustrate: In comparing the effectiveness of several resettlement operations, it is important to know whether, for example, the quality of the soil in one area was the primary factor in the success of one project as compared to another.[2]

Paraphrasing General Wellington's comment on the quality of the troops London had just sent him, this American-Latin American military invasion of the field of agriculture may not scare the Brazilian farmers, but it certainly scares the hell out of me! If the record is disturbing in terms of the military role in United States society, it is no less disturbing in terms of the role we may be encouraging the Latin American military to take in their societies. Defense Department-sponsored research in non-military fields has been curtailed since the date of the hearings quoted from. However it is much more difficult to curtail non-military activities of the military in Latin America.

2. *Ibid.*

17. Aid and Democracy

THE ALLIANCE FOR PROGRESS addressed itself not only to Latin America's economic problems but to its political problems as well. "This Alliance is established on the basic principle that free men working through the institutions of representative democracy can best satisfy Man's aspirations . . . ," the governments said in the Declaration to the People of America which accompanied the Alliance. And they added, "No system can guarantee true progress unless it affirms the dignity of the individual which is the foundation of our civilization."

The statements were signed by representatives of countries with democratically elected governments and, with equal good grace, by representatives of governments that were frank dictatorships.

This dedication to democracy, linked as it was to a continent-wide development program based squarely on aid from the government of the United States, posed a delicate question for the Kennedy administration. The question was what role, if any, should the United States government play in fostering democracy in the Latin American countries other than assisting, or trying to assist, economic and social improvement, and hoping that success in those fields would be accompanied by political improvement.

What should it do about Brazil, the mightiest nation in South America, with a history of military interference in politics? Or about Argentina, with its more flagrant military interference? Were there real and desirable alternatives to those interferences, and if there were, did the United States have an obligation or a right to support them? What should be done about Mexico, with its one-party system which may remind us more of Tito's Yugoslavia than of the United States, but that so far seems to work?

Should the United States try to tell governments and people in the Latin American countries how to behave politically? How would we know what to tell them, and what good would come from telling them? Isn't democracy a home-grown plant? Wouldn't it be mischievous and unhelpful to meddle in the politics of other countries no matter how excellent our intentions should be?

There was a strong impulse to help of course. The Kennedy administration was ideological and activist, and it had the confidence that derives from inexperience. Its instinct, when it saw a problem at home or abroad, was to do something about it. And arranging for free men to work through the institutions of representative democracy throughout Latin America certainly presented a problem. But wouldn't action by the United States government in the political field constitute intervention, especially if it were not requested or consented to by the Latin American government or governments?

Article 15 of the Charter of the Organization of American States says: "No State or group of States has the right to intervene, directly or indirectly, for any reason whatever, in the internal or external affairs of any other State." Similar injunctions against intervention are contained in other treaties and engagements subscribed to by the United States and the other American republics and of course are binding upon them.

Furthermore the Latin American governments had given more importance to nonintervention than they had given to aid. President Franklin D. Roosevelt's Good Neighbor Policy had marked the greatest advance, to date, in our relations with the Latin American countries, and the key to its success was our commitment to nonintervention. More recently, in the various inter-American meetings held to discuss Castro and Castroism, Latin Americans had stressed nonintervention, and it was clear that many of them meant nonintervention by the United States as well as by Cuba or the Soviet Union. Nor were the cases where we had lapsed in carrying out our nonintervention commitment, or where we might be considered to have lapsed, encouraging in their results.

When Juan Domingo Peron was a candidate for election to the Presidency of Argentina, in the 1940's, Spruille Braden, our ambassador in Buenos Aires, who was a political appointee with compulsive ideological and activist tendencies, expressed public disapproval of his candidacy. Far from damaging Mr. Peron's standing this intervention on the part of a foreign representative produced support for Peron among many who didn't favor him, and Peron was elected handily.

Our covert intervention in Guatemala, during the Eisenhower administration, had helped to evict a regime that was threatening to deliver Guatemala over to communism, but the episode left a bad taste in the mouths of Latin Americans and of some Americans as well.

The problem that the Kennedy administration faced was how to promote democracy in the Latin American countries directly and helpfully without being charged with violating our nonintervention pledge, and without feeling, itself, that it was violating the pledge.

As a possible way out of this dilemma persons in the administration revived an old and discredited theory, one, interestingly enough, that Ambassador Braden had invoked to justify his interventions in the political life of Argentina. According to this theory the traditional distinction between intervention and nonintervention now is unreal, since the United States is so big and so powerful that whatever it does vis-à-vis another country constitutes intervention in the sense that it has effects in the country; indeed the United States intervenes even when it does nothing, since doing nothing also has its effects.

Mr. Richard M. Bissell, of the Central Intelligence Agency, who was in charge of planning for the Bay of Pigs invasion and who was decorated by President Kennedy a year after the event, bluntly expressed this theory in a press interview published in the July 21, 1965 issue of the Washington *Evening Star* when he said, "This [the Bay of Pigs] is a distasteful form of intervention, but we have been intervening in the affairs of countries all over the world for years. The Marshall Plan was certainly the most massive form of intervention since World War II."

Now, aside from the grotesque absurdity of comparing the Bay of Pigs episode with the Marshall Plan, Mr. Bissell's theory has a very grave flaw. Patently if everything we do is intervention then nothing we may decide to do is intervention in the traditional sense, and the United States, no less than the Soviet Union, is free to use its awesome power vis-à-vis foreign countries, and within foreign countries, in ways that it and it alone may decide are helpful.

Since the Kennedy administration clearly was on the side of virtue, this weakness in the theory did not appear to bother it, if indeed it recognized it. It would have seriously bothered our neighbors in Latin America, however, if it had been openly proclaimed but it was not. Where it was proclaimed was in the higher circles of the United States government and in the various schools where government officials are trained in national security matters.

One act of virtue that some of our ideologists hoped to accomplish was to "get rid of the oligarchs" in Latin America in order that the "peaceful revolution" our government wished for might be accomplished. Another of course was to get rid of the dictatorships, or at least discourage them in ways that might be open to us.

President Kennedy took very seriously the Alliance's commitment to democracy, even though it was evident to persons familiar with Latin America that, to the signers, or to many of them at least, democracy was an ideal to be pursued, but frequently at a distance; that a democracy that had not been achieved in one hundred and fifty years of effort would not come about overnight as the result of commitments by government representatives meeting at a summer resort in Uruguay.

The Kennedy administration denied, or better delayed, diplomatic recognition to revolutionary regimes in Latin America that did not meet its approval, and it suspended aid to those regimes (although in nonideological fashion it promptly recognized and continued aid to revolutionary regimes it approved). When a regime to which we were denying recognition and aid did something we thought it ought to do, such as calling elections or promising to call them, persons in our government sometimes boasted, and our press boasted more loudly, that it was a result of *our* good work—of American "pressure." It rarely seemed to occur to those who took this view that the regime might have decided to do the thing on its own—that it might have done it despite our attitude, rather than because of it, and despite the risk that we would claim credit for it; that what regimes seek in any country is approval by their own people, which is rarely gained by appearing to give in to foreign pressure.

But the feeling that we were influencing political developments helpfully was sincere and persistent. More than one United

States government official compared the number of revolutions and *coups d'état* in Latin America during the Kennedy administration—one of them was heard to say "under the Kennedy administration"—with the number during the Eisenhower administration in order to determine which of the two presidents had the better score. That of course is like claiming victory for the Detroit Tigers when it is the Pirates and the Mets, in another league, who have been playing.

President Kennedy's ambassador to Peru, a prominent member of Americans for Democratic Action, openly supported one of the candidates in Peru's presidential elections. After his position in Peru had become untenable, he was rewarded by being given a post on another continent.

When the Peruvian military interrupted the electoral process by turning out the government then in office, President Kennedy felt that their action was an affront to the government of the United States as well as to the other American governments that had subscribed to the Alliance for Progress. A White House statement of July 19, 1962, said,

The President has noted developments in Peru with great concern. It is his belief that the action taken by the Peruvian military to depose a democratic, constitutional government has contravened the common purposes inherent in the Inter-American System and most recently restated in the Charter of Punta del Este, which the former Government of Peru and other hemispheric republics pledged to support a year ago. At that historic meeting, the signatories agreed to work together for the social and economic welfare of the hemisphere within a framework of developing democratic institutions.

Our statements and our actions had no helpful effect in Peru. But they were pleasing to ideologists in the United States, and to our press of course, and our government was able to take credit for "supporting" democracy in Latin America. And, to a lesser degree it is true, we continue to take credit for supporting democracy in Latin America, when frequently we may be going through motions that at the best are meaningless and at the worst harmful to the very democracy we claim to be supporting.

Whenever there is an arbitrary change of government in a Latin American country our government still feels that somehow the United States is involved. In a kind of Palovian reaction it suspends aid and recognition and instructs the hapless American ambassador to try to get a promise from the new government that it will call elections in a month, or a year, or sometime at any rate. When the new government hints delicately that elections in its country are none of our business and declines to give us a commitment, we search for it in newspapers and periodicals, including the local version of *Mad* magazine, and when we find something that sounds like a promise, we seize upon it as justification for renewing relations and resuming aid. By that time we are more anxious to extend recognition and aid to the new regime than the regime is to receive them.

The temptation to try to influence the political process in Latin America as a means of hastening economic development is very great. That temptation grows as frustration at the meager results of large-scale aid grows. Persons in Washington now realize what any traveling salesman in Latin America knew forty years ago: that political obstacles to development are greater than economic obstacles.

Possible ways of extending this new kind of aid seem to be tantalizingly open to us. The money needed to affect political developments in Latin America—a few millions here, a few there—is "peanuts," to use a favorite expression of the Washington bureaucracy. And we have an overt and a covert apparatus in our government ready and eager to help. A senior AID official, a dedicated, high-minded man, said to me, a few years ago, "I think one of our major objectives now should be to bring about improvement in the political processes in Latin America." Even the Pentagon, or perhaps I should say especially the Pentagon, has shown an interest in studying the behavioral patterns of Latin Americans.

The Congress has sanctioned and even called for a certain amount of "participation" by the United States government in improving democracy in Latin America. Our AID legislation requires that in administering aid "emphasis shall be placed on assuring maximum participation in the task of economic development on the part of the people of the developing countries, through the encouragement of democratic private and local governmental institutions."[1] The language of this provision is vague enough

1. *Foreign Assistance Act of 1961 as Amended*, chap. 2, title 9, sec. 218.

and broad enough to cover a good deal of intervention on the part of United States officials who may be anxious to promote democratic "revolution" in countries receiving aid.

Aid embodies many of the features of colonialism. No country, as no individual, gets something for nothing, and perhaps the new kind of aid that some have been thinking of is a logical projection of past aid. At any rate, there are persons in and out of government who tend to believe that people can be manipulated for their own good if only we can discover the rules for manipulating them. If the ideas of those persons should take hold, then a new colonialism, no less real than the old, and more pernicious because it is less frank and less responsible, might well emerge.

There is another question related to democracy's future in Latin America, and that is the degree to which our aid program may have encouraged Latin American governments to favor public enterprise over private enterprise. As already noted, the Chilean government, which has a long history of favoring state enterprise, has been a privileged recipient of United States aid. As noted also, that government has embarked on a program aimed at converting the country's enormous copper mining industry, which has been owned and operated by American private interests, into a state-owned enterprise. There is no doubt that resources supplied by the United States government have served to release other resources that the Chilean government feels it can apply to the program.

But public enterprise, like government planning, broadens the field in which political decisions and events have their effects. The Latin American countries have had limited success in insulating state-owned enterprises from politics, and it is not probable that great success in doing that will be achieved easily or soon, if indeed it is ever achieved. Meanwhile, will the industrial bureaucracy as well as the political bureaucracy have to be largely changed when and if a new government comes into power in a Latin American country? Professor Gordon, as we have seen, implies that this is likely to be the case. And if it is, what effect will that have on economic development, and on related political development?

Of course emphasis on state enterprise may reduce the chance that a nation will have the opportunity to bring a new government into power democratically. In that event the problem takes on an added dimension. State enterprise gives to an increasing percentage of people who have jobs in the public sector that they don't want to give up, and usually cannot afford to give up, a direct and even a proprietary interest in who is going to be president, in what political party is going to be in power, indeed in whether the party in office should give up power in any circumstances. Among the most interested, of course, are the armed forces, already traditional arbiters in the political process, whose members, active as well as retired, are finding more and more lucrative jobs in the burgeoning public sector.

It is at least possible that a government that has the power to act as government and also as principal entrepreneur, even though it is less than efficient in either role, is a government that is too powerful for the liberties of its citizens. Argentina, where many and huge state enterprises have been conducted with dramatic inefficiency and disregard for the public weal, may have reached that stage already. Chile may be approaching it.

With the Mexican government owning and operating the ten largest enterprises in the country, and many smaller enterprises as well, is it likely that the present one-party system in the country can be changed without violence and without disruption of the economic as well as the political order?

The Inter-American Development Bank, to which the United States government is the major contributor, is helping to finance a government-owned power plant on the Paraguayan side of the Parana River, which will be large enough to supply power not only to Paraguay but also to Misiones Province in Argentina and Parana in Brazil. No other investment in Paraguay, public or private, will compare with this plant in value. There may be persons in Washington who believe that the political party which has already kept itself in office in Paraguay more than twenty years without the formality of free elections, will peaceably turn over control of such a plant, as well as of the government, with all that both imply in terms of political and economic power and patronage, to another party, but I would estimate that no member of the opposition in Paraguay harbors the illusion that this will occur in his lifetime.

It may well be that there is no present alternative to an increase in public enterprise in Latin America and a related decline in the level of democracy in that area. But if it should appear that that is the case, our government might do well to consider what its relationship to those developments should be. It would be ironic indeed if we should expose ourselves to the charge of intervention in Latin America's internal political affairs by criticizing and imposing sanctions on those we consider are acting undemocratically while we ourselves are contributing to the difficulties that lie in the way of a real and effective democracy in the area.

18. TOPSY and BALPA

TOPSY is the name given in the State Department to the planned reduction of the American official presence in Brazil which, like Topsy, "growed" until it became a bloated caricature of diplomacy.

Some two years ago our then ambassador to Brazil, Mr. John W. Tuthill, who has had a great deal of experience in the aid field, submitted a reasoned report to the Department of State suggesting that the official American presence in Brazil be reduced from nearly a thousand persons to some five hundred. The reductions would have to be made principally in our economic and military assistance programs.

Ambassador Tuthill considered that with half the complement of official Americans that he then had he could do a better job of advancing the interest of the United States in Brazil, and of advancing the interest of Brazil as well. The ambassador suggested further that if he were permitted to organize the kind of "ideal" embassy that he visualized as possible, with the ambassador having greater authority to make decisions on matters of local significance, and greater flexibility in using personnel from the State Department and other agencies, he could do a still better job with a small fraction of the five hundred persons he would have when his staff had been reduced by one-half.

That is an arresting thought, isn't it? What is a small percentage of five hundred? Ambassador Tuthill didn't say. Is 10 percent a small percentage? Ten percent of five hundred is fifty. Is 20 percent a small percentage? Twenty percent of five hundred is one hundred. The ambassador appeared to be suggesting that his embassy and the programs it conducts and supervises could serve the United States and Brazil better with perhaps one hundred or one hundred and fifty Americans than with the one thousand he was authorized to have on his roll when he sent his report in to Washington.

When TOPSY was set in motion there were 934 job slots for official Americans in Brazil. Of these, 748 were in AID, USIA, and the military. In contrast the State Department, which according to the textbooks conducts our foreign relations, had 118 slots, but many Foreign Service officers such as the labor attaché, the minerals attaché, and their assistants, performed services for agencies other than State. And still others spent much of their time supervising and providing services for the 748 program personnel.

There were 479 Americans in AID alone, and it could no longer be concealed that Brazilians had developed a kind of neurosis from being told by these hundreds of Americans what to do in circumstances with which the Americans might be only vaguely familiar, with the result that Aid, despite its great cost to the United States and to Brazil as well, was having effects that perhaps were more harmful than helpful.

Brazil is a country at peace, and is not threatened by any nation. But when TOPSY was undertaken, there were 213 highly visible American military personnel in the country, together with families, cars, PX, and commissary. The United States Navy had a radio station in Brazil which maintained twenty-four hour-a-day communication with the United States. The station employed twenty-six Americans and twenty-six Brazilians. It must have cost nearly as much to operate as our entire diplomatic establishment in Brazil cost not many years before. Whereas communication between government departments in Washington was curtailed during the latest riots in that city, communication between the Pentagon and its representatives in Brazil remained intact. But to what purpose? No one seemed to know.

Ambassador Tuthill was not the first chief of mission in Brazil to complain about excessive personnel and excessive undertakings. One of his predecessors, Ambassador Ellis Briggs, made the same complaint in caustic messages to the State Department, but after he departed for another post the number of Americans in Brazil increased rapidly.

It is not easy, even today, when fiscal and balance of payments problems weigh heavily upon our government, to reduce our representation abroad. When TOPSY was undertaken, the

United States military had four planes with their crews permanently stationed in Brazil. They complained that reductions under TOPSY might force them to give up one or two of the planes, and that they might also require curtailment in the size of the PX and APO facilities. Rumor has it that the ambassador was able to contemplate all these possibilities with equanimity.

One difficulty in the way of reducing staff is that the people in the field who must recommend reductions may be recommending themselves out of jobs, and the people in Washington who approve reductions may be adding to the large number of officers who already are walking the corridors of the State Department, USIA, and AID, looking for jobs, including the jobs now held by those who are approving the reductions.

When TOPSY cuts began, Ambassador Tuthill already had brought about sizeable reductions in staff by failing to fill authorized positions. Later an additional 16 percent were cut and returned to reality, to the United States that is. State Department officials I have talked to consider that a further cut of not less than 18 percent is called for. It will be interesting to see whether the Nixon administration, which needs so urgently to economize, will make such a cut. It remains to be seen also whether the administration and the Congress will go beyond such reductions to the "ideal" embassy Ambassador Tuthill and most career ambassadors yearn for, a slimmed down embassy that will be an efficient instrument of diplomacy but that, until recently, popular wisdom considered could not do the job.

So much for trailblazer TOPSY. What about BALPA?

BALPA was a far broader "reducing exercise" than TOPSY. BALPA stands for Balance of Payments and is the name applied to the exercise which President Johnson ordered on January 18, 1968, after a great deal of prodding by the Congress. BALPA's purpose was to bring about reductions of not less than 10 percent in American personnel of all diplomatic missions throughout the world with staffs of one hundred or more, and substantially larger reductions in ten countries with very large missions. The president also ordered an intensive and long overdue review of United States government activities in all countries. BALPA accounted for an 18 percent reduction in the American official presence abroad.

TOPSY was aimed at increasing the effectiveness of our diplomatic establishment, although obviously the economies it also has brought about are dramatic. BALPA, on the other hand, was made necessary by our critical balance of payments problem, although there can be little doubt that reductions in dollars spent abroad will be accompanied by greatly increased effectiveness. The road we have traveled in the assistance field is not the road we started on. Where did we go astray?

Programs are a means to an end. But programs require a bureaucracy and they require appropriations, and when they get them they acquire a momentum of their own. If aid in principle is good, and if people are required to administer aid, then more aid and more people become program objectives. When that occurs the program itself has become an end, and the end for which the program was devised may be submerged and neglected. The result is not more but less aid. It also may be no aid at all. It may even be the opposite of aid.

Programs, like people, have their own character. They can be important to our foreign policy objectives. They also can be a form of escapism, even of isolationism. A program may mean that we turn our international problems over to technologists and technicians, give them a few billion dollars, and then go back to our normal business of polluting the air and water around us and creating other grievous problems for ourselves at home.

President Kennedy's Alliance for Progress, as we have seen, was a warmed over, condimented version of President Eisenhower's economic program for Latin America. And President Eisenhower's program, aimed at containing Castroism outside Cuba, was a substitute for adequate action against Castro inside Cuba.

Programs may be a form of escapism not only for the country but also for those who engage in them, as the Peace Corps may be and, let's be honest, a diplomatic career as well. Solving the problems of other peoples places us on a higher level than they. We feel superior, detached, almost uninvolved. Our work may take us to the *favelas* of Brazil or the *callampas* of Chile, but it takes us away from the grime of our own ghettos and the inanities of our television culture, which bother us more. And we can be comfortable at the same time. It took me more than a week to get to my first post at Tampico, Mexico. Now you can fly down to Rio in a few hours and get the same shrimp cocktail and filet mignon for lunch that you get on a domestic flight. These things give you a glow, a feeling of living at home, of staying close to the womb, while doing good abroad. Our military technicians abroad have their PXs, their commissaries, domestic postage rates, and, as is inevitable, civilians are demanding equal rights and frequently getting them. Foreigners may hate us for having these exceptional privileges, but this apart, they make living pleasant if not necessarily useful.

The Argentine statesman Domingo Sarmiento once said that Argentina is so rich in agriculture that it can offer a banquet to the world. And he did not exaggerate. So the American embassy in Buenos Aires has a commissary. The hordes of Americans who conduct our programs, and American diplomats as well, invade the commissary in an avid search for American flour, raisins in their bran, push-button shaving cream, and duty-free liquor. Alienating people with conspicuous consumption has to a considerable degree displaced diplomacy.

In many countries where we have assistance programs Americans are so numerous and they live on such a different scale of comfort that they have come to form a colony apart, a kind of foreign enclave that is more and more self-sufficient and less and less in communication with those whom we say we want to help. Reducing these colonies by 50 percent or more and closing their PXs and commissaries might be the best way to help in today's circumstances. If it is argued that many Americans will not go abroad under those conditions, I would say, "so be it." We would be left with the more motivated and they are the only ones who can serve us well in any event.

So what do TOPSY and BALPA mean? They mean drastic cuts in our overseas programs and, even more important, a hard new look at the whole concept of diplomacy by program. And of course we cannot accomplish those things without reexamining and reevaluating our total posture in the world.

Reexamination and reevaluation have long been overdue. Many ambassadors have urged that we halt the senseless proliferation of programs, the increase in the number of American "bodies," as the administrators call them, who are sent abroad to work and live and eat and drink, and occupy houses at exhorbitant rentals, which hard-eyed landlords quickly learn to apply also to the natives whom we say we are helping. Many Foreign Service officers have warned of the risks from inflated programs and many more would have warned of those risks if they had been consulted. But they were not.

TOPSY and BALPA have been the subject of a great deal of comment, much of it underground, on the part of Foreign Service officers in Washington. One anonymous Foreign Service officer has revealed an apocryphal article written for the winter issue, A.D. 2248, of the *Journal of Comparative Philology*. The author says, among other things,

> Several of my colleagues have noted the occurrence of a word-family in a number of world languages that is treaceable to the root *balp*. One school of thought believes that it comes from the jargon of a sport that was popular at that time in the Western hemisphere and Japan, viewing it as a corruption of the word "ballpark" [from American English dialect]. Since the *balp* family of words connotes violence it could, indeed, be connected with a contact sport such as baseball is believed to have been. On the other hand, some of my colleagues view the root as a contraction of the early American phrase "bollixed up." Again, this explanation is plausible, in that most attestations of the word connote confusion and uncertainty.

Like many learned articles this one makes a point. There is no doubt that, to a considerable degree, our assistance programs have been "bollixed up" and that confusion and uncertainty regarding programs have been pervasive in Washington and in many other parts of the world.

But TOPSY and BALPA offer great hope that confusion and uncertainty may be reduced. It is dawning on even the most isolated and sanguine of our program makers that communication, which is another name for diplomacy, is more important to the success of programs than money and "bodies"; that if a program is to succeed in a foreign country it must not be an American program at all but a program of the other country in which the United States, with its vast experience in its own environment and its genuine desire to be helpful, can have a role that perhaps is more limited than at present but also more useful.

PROGRESS

---

19. The Objective

Aid is here to stay. We can increase it or we can reduce it. We can praise it or we can criticize it. We have done all those things in the past and we doubtless shall do them in the future. But one thing we cannot do is to eliminate it—not if we are to act rationally that is.

The economic and military strength of the United States is not equaled by that of any other nation. But it is matched by the dangers that we face in an international world that has more the characteristics of a jungle than of an ordered community.

And our strength is not ours alone. It rests on the strength of other peoples and their willingness to live in a cooperative relationship with us. We are more and more a have-not nation. Our ability to progress in peace as well as to make war depends in part on imports of many materials that we do not produce, or that we produce in insufficient quantities. But we require more than material support from other nations. We require political support and moral support as well. We are not an island nor can we ever be one.

How can we achieve the support and the aid of other nations that we require? We cannot achieve them through coercion. Coercion is contrary to our nature and to our purposes. It would mean abandoning within ourselves one of the aims we seek to achieve throughout the world. And it would not work. We are not omnipotent or nearly so. If we are to achieve our aims it must be through cooperation.

Aid is a form of cooperation. Indeed cooperation is a better name for it than aid. It has no "something for nothing" connotation, and it more aptly describes the phenomenon we have in mind. Aid's purpose is to help preserve or create the kind of world in which we can live in freedom and in reasonable prosperity. A country that receives aid or cooperation, and utilizes it, contributes as much to achieving that purpose as we contribute by offering aid.

If those things are true, and I have no doubt they are, our objective, wherever it may lead us, should be neither to increase aid nor to decrease it but to improve it, to make it more capable of contributing to the worldwide objectives that we share with other free nations and with nations that aspire to be free. And the experience we and the Latin Americans have acquired can help if we both are prepared to learn from it.

20. Trade

Aid is a relatively new concept. It therefore is exciting. It engages our emotions. Intellectually we know that aid is aimed at serving American interest. Emotionally we are aware that it is intended to serve others. Aid rewards with a feeling of self-righteousness as trade never can. If that self-righteousness often is annoying to those we try to help it nevertheless can be satisfying to us. Aid lends itself to oratory, to talk about "common traditions," about "brotherhood," about improving the conditions of the oppressed and the disadvantaged. Speeches on aid make headlines. Speeches on trade may be reported only in the Congressional Record.

Trade is prosaic. It does not arouse the imagination, although it used to in a simpler age when sailing ships rounded the Horn to reach China, and people marveled at the exotic products they brought from little-known places. When I went to school, Tyre and Sidon were places many of us longed to see. We associated them with trade, with land routes to Persia and sea routes to Iberia, with man's communication with man, with the intermingling of peoples and cultures. There is little sail today. Young people hear less of Tyre and Sidon. Nor do the modern ports of New York and Baltimore convey the same sense of romance that Marblehead and Boston once did.

Aid makes it possible to help the oppressed and the disadvantaged, but trade does too, in ways that are basic. Trade makes it possible for countries to help themselves. It also makes it possible for other countries to help, to extend aid that is. And it doesn't require a costly bureaucracy to administer. Trade is a two-way process. Aid can be one-way. It can be granted or withheld at our option. It gives us "leverage" to encourage nations that accept it to conduct themselves, in the economic and social fields, and sometimes in the political field, in ways that we consider desirable. At least we hope it does.

Trade is associated with money-making, a process that many of us deprecate in principle while we avidly engage in it in fact. It demands long experience and expert attention if it is to be carried on profitably. In contrast, almost anyone can be an expert in aid because there are no experts in the field. And failure to accomplish the purposes of aid, failure to "make a profit," can always be blamed on the Congress' parsimoniousness or on the unexplainable reluctance of other peoples to act as we wish them to act.

Like other things that are not new or exciting, trade tends to be taken for granted. The coffee from distant Brazil that we buy in the supermarket is wrapped in a package that is as aseptic and as smart as the package Wisconsin cheese comes in, and usually easier to open. Bananas are on the shelves so constantly that they might well be produced in the next county instead of in the steaming flatlands of Colombia and Honduras.

But trade is not taken for granted by those who engage in it or by others, at home and abroad, who know that it is more important than aid, that it is a nation's life blood no less. Most nations could live reasonably satisfactory lives, in their own terms if not in ours, with a minimum of aid, or even no aid, from abroad. Many would slip back into primitive barbarism if trade should disappear or be greatly diminished. Happily trade is continuous. It is carried on by private persons and groups in the tradition of free societies. It does not depend on annual appropriations of the United States Congress. Rather it contributes to the support of the Congress and of our government in general, and of other governments as well. It is an indispensable element in that support.

Trade tempers animosities. It links people together. It converts many and disparate nations into one world. It transcends politics, although not completely. Nothing transcends politics completely. Politics, as a rule, cannot cancel trade as it can aid, but it can affect it. Tariffs and import quotas can limit trade. They also can limit and even negate the effects of aid. And the possibility that this will occur merits as much thought as aid itself does. Probably more.

The United States has come a long way since 1930, the year the Smoot-Hawley Tariff Act imposed excessively high duties on imports and made its own contribution to worldwide depression and war. Beginning with Cordell Hull's Reciprocal Trade Agreements Program and continuing through the Kennedy Round, our record has been good; better perhaps than that of any other large nation. Our record vis-à-vis Latin America has been especially good.

Although some of Latin America's products, notably petroleum, are subject to import restrictions most of its exports enter the United States freely. In addition we pay premium prices for sugar imports under our long-standing sugar legislation, and higher prices for coffee as a result of the World Coffee Agreement, which we helped to sponsor. It has been estimated that aid to Latin America in the form of higher prices for those two products may amount to some five hundred or six hundred million dollars a year. It soon may be more extensive than conventional aid, if the latter continues to be reduced by a skeptical Congress.

Aid in the form of higher prices is not usually stressed by aid enthusiasts. For one thing it does not give us the same leverage to affect developments in the countries we help. But Latin American exporters like it for reasons that are obvious. And Latin American governments like it too. They probably would have settled for higher export prices at Bogotá in 1960. The Act of Bogotá was more our idea than it was theirs. Aid in the form of higher prices does have merit. It gives governments greater freedom to handle their own affairs—to decide themselves how they will try to influence the creation and distribution of wealth in their countries. And only through practice in handling their own affairs will governments become expert and responsible.

There are limits to this kind of aid of course. For us sugar is a special case, closely related to domestic sugar production and domestic politics. Coffee is a special case too, because of its importance to the economy of Latin America and of other portions of the underdeveloped world. Possibilities of stabilizing or improving the prices of other Latin American products may be meager. Nor are they without risks. Among these is the risk that with assured prices for certain products Latin American countries will fail adequately to diversify their economies, that they will continue to depend inordinately on one crop or on a few crops, and on year-to-year politics in the United States.

While our record in the treatment of international trade is good there nevertheless is a real and imminent danger that we will slip back into protectionism; not the protectionism of the Smoot-Hawley era perhaps, but a protectionism broad and extensive enough to lessen appreciably the effects of foreign aid. This seemed unlikely a few years ago but war, unbalanced budgets, foreign exchange deficits, and rising production costs have served to revive pressures to limit or further limit a wide range of imports that include textiles from Colombia and Argentina, cotton from Peru, and strawberries and tomatoes from Mexico.

Congress is especially vulnerable to protectionist pressure. The same congressman who votes for aid without penalty from his constituents may risk defeat at the next election if he fails to vote protection for goods that are produced in his district. Nevertheless Congress, in the main, has held the line against protectionist pressures. And President Johnson was frequently ready with the veto in case it did not hold the line. But pressures are increasing. Will other Congresses and other presidents be as helpful? There is no assurance that they will.

Continued reduction in aid to Latin America might or might not have the effects in Latin America that many fear. But reduction in aid plus reduction in trade could have catastrophic effects. An aid program, even one at present levels, that was accompanied by a return to protectionism would make no sense. At the best it would be a form of "conscience money," at the worst a form of hypocrisy. It also would be self-defeating.

21. The Problem

QUITE A FEW YEARS AGO an American company obtained a concession to exploit a large area of tropical pine in the Central American republic where I was serving. Since ships could not dock in the open roadstead that was to serve the company as harbor, the project involved devising a special system for placing the timber aboard vessels for export. After careful consideration, the company decided that the logs should be dumped into the sea and floated out to the vessels. Equipment to carry out the operation was prepared and brought down from the United States.

Appropriate ceremonies were arranged to inaugurate the new venture. The president of the company came down from New Orleans aboard the ship that was to carry back the first load of logs. A representative of His Excellency, the President of the Republic, made the arduous journey overland from the nation's capital to give testimony of the government's enthusiasm for the project, which promised to help improve the country's precarious balance of international payments. Local officials and citizens were present in great numbers. Speeches were made. A military band, resplendent in new uniforms, was there to give added drama to the occasion.

At a given signal a tiny locomotive gingerly pushed a flatcar loaded with logs onto the pier that had been constructed for the purpose. The band struck up a martial tune, the car was tilted, and the logs rolled off into the sea. They promptly sank. The company's plan to float the logs out to vessels for loading was based on the assumption that Central American pine behaves as American pine behaves. But the Central American pine insisted perversely on behaving as Central American pine behaves.

To many persons who read the press and watch television, and I might add, to some persons who have contributed to making policy toward the countries of Latin America, the Latin American problem is disarmingly simple, as simple as floating logs out to sea.

Latin America has low living standards. Its people want those standards raised. They want to eat better, dress better, live better. They want improved education for their children. They are embarked on what some of our orators call a revolution of rising expectations. In order to carry out that revolution they want our cooperation. We are in a position to extend cooperation and we are in fact already extending a great deal through our economic and technical assistance programs, although not enough apparently. Clearly then, if we would cooperate more, presumably by having bigger programs, better coordinated programs, or programs that permit long term planning, Latin America's problems would be solved and the continent would be saved from communism. Conversely if we don't cooperate more, the problems won't be solved, communism may triumph, and blame will rest largely on us.

Lately, as we have seen, another condition for success has been emphasized. That is that the Latin Americans should step up their own efforts in the process; that, among other things, they should embark on programs of reform, and we have helped select the areas in which reform should take place.

All this is equivalent to saying that if Americans do all they are capable of doing to help the Latin American countries, and if Latin Americans do all they should do to help themselves, the problem of development will be promptly solved. But nearly all human problems would be solved if human beings did all they should do to solve them. Why, then, do so many problems go unsolved? Why do some of Latin America's problems worsen despite earnest efforts on the part of our government to help solve them?

The Marshall Plan was the first and by far the most successful of our large-scale aid programs, and its success is not apt to be duplicated in circumstances that we can envisage today. Whereas the problem of European recovery and reconstruction was urgent and of vast dimensions, its solution, in retrospect, was comparatively simple. Large areas of Western Europe had been devastated by war, but most of the physical plant remained intact. More important still, Europe possessed a reservoir of experience, traditions, and skills that were the accumulation of centuries. When the United States was able to add a small percentage of aid, over and above what Europe itself was able to provide, our contribution acted as a catalytic agent, and the European countries, helped by a newly found ability to cooperate with each other as well as with us, restored their economies rapidly.

But our task of cooperating with the underdeveloped countries is infinitely more complex. Indeed it is only beginning to be understood. Basically, of course, the problem in Europe was one of reconstruction, of restoring modern, sophisticated economies that had been long in developing. What our government is trying to do in many of the Latin American countries is to help them reach a point that Europe reached a century or more ago, after earlier centuries of effort and training. Europe has been the home and the fountain of material progress. In many of the Latin American countries there is little understanding of what material progress involves.

The miracle of Europe was Europe's miracle. But other areas are not in a position to perform miracles. We were helping Europe to do what it had already demonstrated it could do. But we are asking the Latin Americans to do things they have not demonstrated they can do. One might go farther, in the cases of some countries, and say that we are asking them to do things they have demonstrated they cannot do—today at least.

All the Latin American countries have material resources capable of being further developed. All of them have the good will of the more developed nations, particularly the United States, whose leaders, I am sometimes tempted to believe, have spent nearly as much time worrying about development in Latin America as have the Latin Americans themselves. How can we improve our assistance to Latin America and how can Latin America place itself in a better position to take advantage of that assistance?

22. Americans

THERE ARE two ways of offering aid to Latin America. One is for the United States government publicly to press the Latin American governments and peoples to do certain things in order to place themselves in a position to receive our aid. That is the method we first employed under the Alliance for Progress. The other is to let the Latin American governments know, quietly, that we are prepared to extend aid to the degree that countries offer promise that it will be usefully employed. That is the method we followed under the Marshall Plan. In my view it is the only method that will work.

Latin American governments do not require our public and private exhortations to know what they should do to help prepare their countries to receive aid. They have many ways of learning what they should do. Many of their own economists can tell them. International institutions such as the World Bank, the International Monetary Fund, and the Inter-American Development Bank, of which the countries are members, will give them frank and useful advice. And of course our own advice will be given, if it is sought.

The difficulty usually is not in knowing what to do. It is in knowing how (and also when) to do it in environments that have impeded progress in the past and that continue to impede it. And that is a difficulty that countries and governments must overcome largely through their own efforts. For us to intercede directly is apt to increase the difficulty. Also it smacks of the colonialism that we deny we practice and that we abhor when we suspect we see it in others.

Dr. Alberto Lleras Camargo, again speaking as a friendly critic, has said "it is evident that as regards legislative reform affecting the domestic and exclusive order of each state, it is an impertinence, to say the least, as well as unnecessary and self-defeating, for such demands to come from the organs of power of another state, from its press, or from its own officials."[1] It was the United States he was referring to of course.

All of us can agree that reform in such fields as taxation and land tenure is needed in Latin America. But true reform, in any country, comes not so much when it is needed, from the economic viewpoint, as when it is possible, or necessary, from the political viewpoint, and it is hazardous for a foreign government, or even an international committee, to decide when that time has arrived.

Prior to the 1930's our government tended to judge reform in the Latin American countries nearly exclusively in the light of its effects on private American interests. There is no question that our more liberal attitude of today marks an advance over our earlier practice. But we should avoid going too far in pressing for reform, or even approving reform, in places where we are not sovereign and where reform, or attempted reform, may lead to results that are quite different from those we have in mind. Reform was needed in Cuba and our government gave Castro reiterated and possibly gratuitous assurance that it appreciated the need of reform. But Cuba today is Communist.

The Alliance for Progress is a frontal attack against ignorance, disease, and poverty in Latin America, and we are the authors and principal sponsors of the Alliance, even though recently we have tried to appear not to be. But it is doubtful that a government should engage in a frontal attack in some one else's country, whether it be against poverty or whatever else it may feel needs correcting. It is not an appropriate tactic for a foreign government, particularly one as powerful as ours, with a historical penchant for intervention. Some persons abroad will not object to it. But others will object and they are apt to include many who are important to us and to the purposes we have in common with the Latin Americans.

Frontal attacks are useful and even necessary in war, but diplomacy, including aid diplomacy, to the extent that it can be compared with war, is more in the nature of a guerrilla operation, where frontal attacks are eschewed. Our aid armies have been given excellent weapons, and there will always be opportunities

---

1. Council of the Organization of American States, Pan American Union, Washington, D. C., *Report on the Alliance for Progress* (OEA/Ser.G/V C-d-1103), 15 June 1963, p. 17.

to use them. Central American governments, as we have seen, have shown a considerable ability to cooperate with each other in fields that are appropriate and helpful. In Central America the enemy, the problem of underdevelopment that is, has been retreating and we have been able to advance with a measure of confidence. The outbreak of hostilities between Honduras and El Salvador may have interrupted this forward trend, but there is reason to hope that progress will be resumed.

Under Mexico's unique and, so far, successful system of one-party government, the disruptions that normally accompany political change in Latin America have been reduced. Government in Mexico may not be efficient, but it has been continuous and relatively dependable. That facilitates cooperation. In some other countries, on the other hand, if the enemy is not advancing, it is standing still, and we can do little more than engage in tactics of harassment.

In the aid field, the frontal attack should be left to the people whose burden we are trying to lighten. The burden is theirs to carry, and we should be careful not to give them the impression we can lift it from their shoulders. They are capable of believing that we can, and if they do, then development will be retarded rather than advanced.

Latin America's desires in the economic and social field will probably never be met to the satisfaction of her people or of her political leaders. For the United States government to assume a major responsibility for seeing that those desires are met, as it did under the Alliance for Progress, was to invite the resentment of persons and groups in Latin America, and that resentment and the results flowing from it were bound to constitute a new impediment to Latin America's progress.

If I were in government I would not mix aid and ideology. I would save my ideology for my own country. We find it easy to preach, but people tire of preachments. Every Latin American people aspires to be democratic. There is no quarrel about aims. Here again the problem is one of means. The Latin Americans think they know more about that than we do, and they may be right. I would try to hold high the banner of democracy but I would not keep mouthing the word. If Latin Americans are capable of achieving democracy they will achieve it without our preachments and without our having to exert political and economic pressure on them.

From time to time, in given countries, there will be conflict between the practice of democracy and the achievement of development, both aims of the Alliance for Progress. When that occurs, one or the other, or both, may be sacrificed, at least temporarily. The pressure to produce more, to satisfy needs and aspirations, a pressure that we have added to in many ways, will remain a threat to democracy until democracy becomes more efficient and more effective. Arbitrary government may not, in practice, be more effective than democratic government, but there will be a hope that it will be, and the hope will bring it about and sustain it in some cases. The Latin American peoples have been trying for one hundred and fifty years to improve their institutions, with varying success, and they will continue to try to improve them. Meanwhile upsets are inevitable. Some of them will be needed. Needed or not, the upsets should not send ideologists in our government into a public dither.

We should avoid taking sides in Latin American politics even though we are convinced we are on the side of virtue. Political contests in Latin America are not contests between good and evil. No political faction, in Latin America any more than in the United States, is ever as pure as it claims to be, and we demean ourselves by taking sides.

We take sides when we interrupt aid in order to force political change in a country. The Alliance for Progress was subscribed to by governments. It was to be carried out by governments in cooperation with one another. Nothing in the Alliance authorizes a government to go over the head of another government and decide what is good for another country or another people. Nothing in the Alliance confers any right upon us to punish Latin American governments for failure to carry out the purposes of the Alliance, or for what we may consider to be failure. The failures of Latin American governments are the failures of Latin American peoples, just as the failures of our government are our failures, and the United States government has no right or reason to punish foreign peoples for their failures or their errors. We are not an imperial power with the authority to punish, nor are the Latin Americans colonial peoples.

We take sides when we blame those whom we have chosen to call oligarchs for problems that have complex origins, and that many oligarchs may understand better than we do. Name-calling is not helpful in any case. It offends individuals. It impugns motives. It strips persons of their patriotism. It stirs up animosity between classes and between persons. It deprives us of the cooperation of people whose cooperation is needed if the ends we seek are to be attained. We should leave name-calling to the Communists and to those who follow them. Their purpose is to tear down. Ours is to help build.

While I would not use or misuse aid in order to affect processes that we are enjoined from interfering with, neither would I continue aid unless it promises to be useful. Aid is an instrument of national policy. That policy, in its objectives at least, is high-minded and enlightened. It equates the true interest of the American people with the true interest of other peoples, and it assumes that economic improvement in the underdeveloped countries is in the American interest as well as in the interest of those countries. But high-minded and enlightened as it undoubtedly is, American policy still is intended to serve American interest, and its instrument, aid, also is intended to serve that interest. It could hardly be justified to our citizens and our taxpayers if that were not the case.

Aid is not something another government may demand as a right and dispose of in ways that it alone may determine. It is not a form of tribute. Unless it encourages and helps a country to improve its own contribution to development, it is apt to do more harm than good, to us as well as to the country receiving it. If aid is having the effect of strengthening tyranny in a given country we have an obligation to review our program, although not necessarily to cancel it. Aid may be helpful to those whom we want to help even though they are living under arbitrary government, and tyranny, like democracy, is interpreted differently by different people, in different places, and at different times.

If the oligarchy insists on retaining ownership of most of the tillable land in a given country then we should bear that clearly in mind in our cooperative relations with that country. If the oligarchs or the demagogues, or both, try to excuse their errors or failures by charging the United States with not helping enough, as they may, it is not beyond the resources of competent diplomacy to turn the tables on them and help place responsibility where it rightfully belongs.

The Bible tells us that we should be not only harmless as a dove but also wise as a serpent, and the advice is nowhere more valid than in the field of diplomacy, including aid diplomacy. It is probably the failure to observe this biblical injunction that makes it difficult for so many do-gooders to do good. We should try to improve the role of government in the development process, but we should be more skeptical of government's role than some of our political leaders have been in recent years. If I sound like a reactionary, it is not that I wish to. On the contrary my instincts are liberal. But facts in Latin America are not the same facts we face in the United States.

I recall that when I was in Argentina, John Kenneth Galbraith, whom no one would accuse of being a conservative, made a swing around South America. He started at the northern tip of the continent and worked his way south. He showed no reluctance to talk to the press and some of the headlines in the newspapers we were reading in Argentina were disquieting. They gave the impression that the eminent economist was recommending that Latin American governments act in the economic field in ways that he thought the United States government should act at home. We needn't have worried. By the time the professor had reached Argentina he was talking less like John Kenneth Galbraith than like Henry Hazlitt. Facts had triumphed over ideology.

It is all very well to say that each country should be free to develop in its own way, as though countries could choose among many ways, but it has been demonstrated that state enterprise, in general, does not work in Latin America—that it retards progress rather than promotes it. If a government's development plan discourages private effort or even fails to encourage it, we should be skeptical of the usefulness of foreign aid no matter how beautifully the plan may be drawn up. If a government wants help from the United States government to set itself up in business, the burden should be on it to demonstrate that the help won't damage rather than promote the country's economy. We have an obligation not to encourage countries in failure.

In its approach to the Alliance for Progress the United States government stressed public investment over private investment.

What it had in mind principally, of course, was Latin America's need for added infrastructure, and under the Alliance large sums have been spent on such common infrastructure as roads, bridges, and power plants, and such social infrastructure as schools, although still not enough to meet Latin America's needs. But infrastructure, like nearly everything else in this world, has to be paid for, and it has to be utilized if it is to be a help rather than a burden. Furthermore, if Latin America is to develop in freedom, infrastructure will be paid for and made productive through the efforts of private persons and groups, Latin American and foreign. It is those efforts that require the special support of the Latin American governments and of the government of the United States as well.

AID Director Bell rightly gave importance to the growing number of development banks that we have helped to set up in Latin America, and of cooperatives and credit unions, all intended to encourage private savings and investment. Administrator Gaud was equally justified in stressing what appeared to him to be an increasing recognition by the middle classes in Latin America of their pivotal role in development. Adequate development in Latin America will require the best efforts of all elements of society, and whatever the United States government can do to support those efforts will constitute aid in the truest sense.

The United States government also urged its Alliance partners to engage in national planning, and most of them went along with enthusiasm. But the private individuals and groups whose activities will determine whether or not plans will succeed have in general been left out of the planning process. In the circumstances, many have become skeptical and suspicious, and even antagonistic toward government planning. Much of what has passed for planning has hindered rather than furthered development in Latin America.

Reports of the Agency for International Development concerning Latin America are replete with references to GNP (gross national product), per capita income, development "needs," and external "requirements," but there is little in them concerning the role of people in development and the attitude of governments toward that role, despite the circumstance that a proper respect by government for the role of people, and adequate support of that role, are among the most urgent requirements of development. It is time our government gave greater attention to those requirements.

Not only should aid be directed preferentially toward private groups; more of it could profitably be carried out by private groups. Government aid has involved the expenditure of vast sums of money and the services of a large bureaucracy. But these are not necessarily the determinants of good aid. No government aid program to Latin America that I am familiar with compares in its results with the Rockefeller Foundation's work in improving corn and wheat production in Mexico. With a very small number of carefully selected Americans and an expenditure in money that was insignificant compared with the cost of many United States government aid projects, the Rockefeller Foundation was able to bring about improvement in Mexico's domestic food supply that was dramatic, to say the least, and in the view of some persons nearly miraculous. And most of the work of improvement was done by Mexicans. The Foundation was responsible for similar although less dramatic improvement in Colombia and Chile.

ADELA, an international investment company organized in order to assist development in Latin America has sparked more than $800 million of private investment in Latin America with an investment of its own of little more than $30 million. Furthermore ADELA has earned a profit, although profit has been merely a by-product of its efforts, tangible evidence that the investments it has helped to bring about have been productive. There is room for ADELA to continue to expand, and room for more ADELAS. They might turn out to be more productive and more important than costly government aid—a hopeful thought in the event the United States Congress continues to reduce aid appropriations.

Representatives of large American and other foreign firms are serving as directors of ADELA. Their purpose is ADELA's purpose—to help Latin Americans meet their development needs. The firms they represent also are helping to meet those needs, in ways that are basic, but their contributions are not so clear as they might be to many. Intellectually many Latin Americans appreciate the help they receive from foreign corporations. Intellectually and emotionally, however, Latin Americans want to strengthen their own role in development, and if progress is to be satisfactory, it is imperative that they should. Foreign companies might help in still other ways to strengthen that role, for example by exploring further the possibility of joint ventures with Latin Americans, and by selling stock in their companies to Latin American investors. A degree of risk that goes beyond short-term commercial considerations might pay off handsomely in the end, for the foreign companies as well as in terms of economic and social progress in Latin America.

Our government has shown an almost morbid interest in the "image" it projects abroad. If there is such a thing as an "image" outside the jargon of Madison Avenue and the United States Information Agency, then a certain preoccupation with the image we project in Latin America is of course desirable, but we should spurn transient and superficial indications of what that image is. A mob that is rioting in Lima or Caracas does not necessarily reflect any image other than its own. And we certainly should not base our concept of the image we are projecting on news reports that are written to sell papers or on statements of politicians, American or foreign, that are intended to be self-serving.

Of course we damage our image the moment we give others the impression we are concerned with it, and excessive talk about the image we project in Latin America has already done us harm. Madison Avenue has little proper place in diplomacy, although its methods are increasingly used. In place of preoccupation with what we appear to be, with our image in other words, I urge greater preoccupation with what we are. A nation preoccupied with what it is rather than what it appears to be projects its own image abroad, perhaps the only image that is enduringly helpful.

In offering aid I would bear in mind that demagogy in Latin America has been a barrier to progress, and I would not add to it by arousing expectations that cannot be met. Rather I would help to combat demagogy in ways that are appropriate.

Education is the enemy of demagogy. AID today is helping to finance programs of cooperation between a large number of American and Latin American universities. Tomorrow's problems in our country will be solved by persons now in school or who soon will be entering school. Cooperation in education helps train Latin Americans to solve their problems, and since they are the only ones who can solve them, education is an ideal field for cooperation.

If education is a fruitful field for cooperation it also is a delicate and difficult field. Educators in the United States are facing problems of their own that will require their closest attention. Some are showing no great success in meeting them. Cooperation with Latin America requires equally close attention and success is equally difficult to achieve. Cooperation in education is not a routine matter. It is not enough to give a contract to a university and hope that it will be able to find men to carry it out. Cooperation in education requires the services of the best of our teachers. "Availability" should not be the criterion for selecting professors as it so often has been in the past. Adding American mediocrity to Latin America's problem will not help solve that problem.

Before our government agreed to help finance the creation of a graduate school of economics at Catholic University in Chile, our aid director discussed the possibility of such a project with every Chilean university that might be capable of carrying it out. Catholic University showed the greatest enthusiasm and offered the greatest prospect of success. But our aid director recommended it only after lengthy and protracted conversations with the president and faculty members and also with groups in Chilean society whose support might be needed to insure the project's success.

In the United States the aid director sought out the one educator he considered most qualified to head up the American end of the project, and that person agreed to give his cooperation and his university's cooperation only after he had made more than one trip to Santiago and had his own conversations with persons and groups he considered important. Finally, when the project was agreed to, only the most carefully selected professors from the United States and professors and graduate students from Chile were permitted to take part. Success in those circumstances was substantially assured before the project was undertaken.

It is not easy for universities in the United States to give that kind of attention to cooperative projects, nor is it easy to find aid directors who will do it, but nothing less will accomplish the job. This inevitably will limit the amount of cooperation we can offer in the educational field. However it also will assure that cooperation will be fruitful. A few dozen fruitful projects at a given time might have dramatic effects in advancing education in Latin America. They might also help to improve education in the United States. A hundred projects carried out by routine men in routine ways might have no such effects.

Progress in education is slow and undramatic. It doesn't lend itself to slogans. But it is continuous and it is assured. Cooperation in education means that Latin American professors and students come to the United States and see us as we are. They see, firsthand, that we too are odd ducks, that we have many problems they may not have heard much about. And they teach people in the United States about their countries. Our scholars learn about Latin America by going there and living there, by studying Latin America's problems, by working on them with Latin Americans, by observing Latin America as it is and not as the books or Latin America's representatives abroad say it is. Our need to learn about Latin America is very great. In most cases we need to learn before we can help. Education is not a cure-all in Latin America any more than in any other area, and Latin America's educational needs are not identical with ours.

A few years ago I visited a large Latin American country and complimented one of my friends, a university rector, on the evident advances the country had made in the educational field. "Yes," my friend observed, "we are in a very dangerous position. The country is filled with half-educated people and we don't know where they will take us."

A president of another Latin American country, also an old friend, told me not long ago that he hoped that professors who came to his country from the United States would have open minds concerning the country's problems until they had an opportunity to familiarize themselves with those problems and with the political and cultural setting in which they existed.

When he said that, I remembered an excellent aid director who served with me in Paraguay (the same director who later served with me in Chile). He told me that it had taken him five years to learn what Paraguay's problems really were. He was a highly intelligent, splendidly educated man. He spoke the two languages that Paraguayans speak. He was there on the spot.

And yet it had taken him five years to learn what Paraguay's problems were.

In contrast, during the early years of the Alliance for Progress more than one White House staff assistant prescribed remedies for Latin America's problems without ever having visited the area and without knowing the people who must carry out the prescriptions.

23. Latin Americans

AND WHAT ABOUT Latin America?

The shortcomings that Latin Americans share with other peoples help to explain their failure to advance at a satisfactory pace, but in the minds of thoughtful Latin Americans they no longer excuse that failure. Those Latin Americans know that their countries must surmount ways and traditions that hamper them if they are even to stand still in relation to the more developed countries. Furthermore they are confident that this can be done. I share their confidence.

While the greatest enemy of progress in Latin America is demagogy, not all Latin Americans are deceived by demagogues, and few are deceived all the time. Latin Americans have had a great deal of experience with demagogues. In some ways they are more sophisticated than our own people are.

My Latin American friends in the United States, and many in Latin America, have no trouble discovering the fallacies of the numerous outrageous statements made during our national political campaigns. They have little trouble discovering our political weaknesses, or their own. These are not average Latin Americans, but there are many like them, capable of leading their countries forward. As individuals these Latin Americans compare favorably with our own people. I recall that an Argentine once asked a member of my staff, "How is it that individually we Argentines are more intelligent than you Americans, but collectively we don't seem to get anywhere?"

One does not have to agree with the assumption of individual superiority, made only partly in jest, in order to agree that Latin Americans have the capacity to learn, to acquire skills, including the most complex, that they need to acquire in order to take their place in today's competitive world. What can they do to insure that they will in fact occupy that place?

I shall not try to tell Latin Americans what they should do. I shall, instead, report the views that Latin Americans of great experience and, I believe, of great wisdom, have expressed to me. For Latin America political and economic development are more than desirable objectives. They have become imperatives.

Governments in Latin America, like governments everywhere, should use their powers and the resources available to them to promote social justice, to improve the lot of the underprivileged, but direct help is not the only kind of help nor is it usually the most effective kind. Direct help is limited by the amount of resources available, and the more needy the country the less adequate are its resources. In the last analysis, more and better homes, improved health and improved education will be achieved only if economies are able to provide them. Economies capable of doing that, to the degree aspired to, do not exist in Latin America today, nor will they be created without aid from the outside—more aid than Latin America is now receiving. Political leaders in Latin America agree with this, but not all of them agree with its implications.

Satisfactory progress in Latin America without the assistance of additional foreign private investment is not conceivable at this stage of history. Latin America has shown no talent for lifting itself up by its own bootstraps, and there is little reason to believe that it will develop any such talent. Puerto Rico, our own small segment of Latin America, made a true "leap forward" through its "Operation Bootstrap," but the key to the Operation's success was massive private investment from continental United States.

The arguments in favor of foreign private investment have become tiresome, nearly as tiresome as Latin America's complaints concerning underdevelopment. Latin Americans are tired of hearing the arguments and others are tired of expressing them. Yet to ignore them is to place in jeopardy the economic goals Latin America aspires to achieve.

Investment by foreign private capital has played a key role in development in the past and its role can be equally useful in the future. It brings with it skills and techniques that are indispensable, and that are more important today, as well as more difficult to acquire, than they ever have been. It does not burden a government's budget. The wealth that foreign investment produces adds to the sum of domestic wealth. It facilitates the accumulation of domestic capital and reduces dependence on foreign capital. The United States has demonstrated this. But foreign capital was welcomed in the United States. Latin America must have an equally rational attitude toward foreign capital if it is to progress.

Some will say that this is an oversimplification. They will point to the risk that foreign capital will be invested in hamburger stands or worse and that remittances of profits will constitute a needless drain on a country's economy. Others will say that foreign-owned factories will drive domestically-owned factories out of business because they are more efficient or because they are content with lower earnings. The size of American corporations remains a problem of course. In Europe many persons are fearful that their societies will be dominated by mammoth American corporations. One can sympathize with that fear. Indeed many Americans have the same fear with reference to their own society. Fear of bigness has been no less real in Latin America.

On the other hand the problem of bigness, as well as other problems that foreign investment gives rise to, may not be beyond the wit of people and governments in Latin America to control. In fact Latin American governments already have demonstrated that they are not helpless to protect their own interest and the interest of citizens.

The Chilean government has had little trouble controlling the foreign copper companies, nor has the Venezuelan government had much trouble controlling the foreign petroleum companies. Those companies are the mainstays of the two countries' economies, and each government has been able to insure that the bulk of the foreign exchange the companies produce, and of the companies' earnings, goes directly to support the country's economy and to increase the government's revenues.

Not all enterprises that might be willing to invest in Latin America are as large as United States Steel or as Sears, Roebuck and Company, and both those large corporations have invested in Latin America without endangering the economies or the politics of the countries that admitted them. Rather they have contributed to economic and social improvement, and probably indirectly to political improvement as well.

If anything, Latin American governments have tended to

overprotect their interests and the interests of citizens. What is called for now may be greater liberality toward foreign investment and, in many cases, toward domestic investment as well. In any event, it is better to have the kinds of problems that foreign investment creates than the problem of poverty and despair that is increasing in Latin America and that is much less susceptible to regulation and control.

But it is not going to be so easy as it once was to attract investment to Latin America. Puerto Rico's task, in comparison, was simple. In addition to tax privileges, Puerto Rico could offer political stability, the protection of American laws, and duty-free access to the American market. Latin America cannot match these. New capital will enter the area in amounts needed, only if a new and extraordinary effort is made to attract it. Promises of governments will no longer suffice.

Nor will investment guarantees extended by the United States government do the job. The mere existence of an investment guarantee program insures that Americans who plan to invest in Latin America will seek guarantees from the United States government, in other words that the program will be used. And what is used is assumed to be useful. But the Latin American countries are not "newly emerged." They have had a century and a half of experience in the responsibilities of nationhood. In those circumstances the need of investment guarantees by a foreign government, or the alleged need, detracts from confidence in Latin America as a place for investment. What would add to confidence are guarantees by Latin American political groups. It is pressure from the opposition, or pressure which the party in office generated when it was in the opposition, that is frequently responsible for the unhelpful attitude toward foreign capital, and toward domestic capital too, that one has noted increasingly in Latin America.

The Chilean Congress, not many years ago, enacted a tax law that encouraged the copper mining companies to make large new investments in the country, but after the investments were made, a new Congress reimposed rates that were discouragingly high. The Chilean government, in 1967, granted the Anaconda Company new franchises covering the operation of its mining enterprises for a period of twenty years. But the same Chilean government swept those franchises aside two years later when it pressed the company to sell its properties under threat of expropriation. The Goulart government in Brazil also showed little respect for the foreign capital that earlier regimes had welcomed.

Argentina's President Arturo Frondizi signed contracts with foreign petroleum companies and welcomed new foreign investment in many other areas. But as we have seen, Frondizi's political opponents, when they took over the government, canceled the contracts and created an atmosphere that was discouraging to both foreign and domestic capital.

As we have seen too, the Belaunde government in Peru agreed to settle a long-standing dispute with a large American company concerning the ownership of a valuable property. However the dispute had become a football of Peruvian politics and the military group that overthrew the Belaunde government promptly denounced the agreement and seized the property.

These attitudes and acts, and other similar acts, have not gone unnoticed. They have come to symbolize the general environment in Latin America, an environment which is not conducive to progress. Foreign capital already in the area can be expected to stay there and to reinvest a large part of its earnings, as it has done in the past, but much more than that is needed. New investments, new industries, are needed and needed quickly.

Latin Americans will agree with this or they will disagree with it. If they disagree, they will do nothing to improve the climate for new foreign investment and little progress will be made despite fine phrases such as Alliance for Progress. If they agree with it, then they must act quickly and more broadly than they have acted in the past. Persons in political life must recognize, publicly and courageously, as many now do privately and timidly, that demagogy solves no problems and creates many. The demagogue will no longer be applauded because he uses the language of patriotism. He will be denounced, as an act of patriotism.

If Brazil's leading political groups when they are free to express themselves should agree that their plans for a better Brazil require the cooperation of private capital and that henceforth foreign as well as domestic capital should be respected and protected, and if they should make known their agreement in that sense, new investment, direct and indirect, would flow into Brazil in amounts that might surprise the most sanguine. Brazil's economy would take on new life, and her democracy also would be strengthened.

If the leading political groups in Argentina should do a similar thing, Argentina, with a potential for development that few countries possess, would leap ahead economically, and Argentina's politics too would be healthier. In a more advanced and more prosperous Argentina, with a larger pie to divide among competing groups, the role of foreign capital would be a less tempting subject for demagogic debate.

Furthermore, if one of those countries should take the step, others would be obliged, in their own interest to follow, and if they did, few Latin American countries would wish not to go along. Each country is sensitive to what goes on in neighboring countries. When President Frondizi was trying to combat inflation in Argentina the then Brazilian government tried, in subtle ways, to discourage him. It was afraid of the effects in Brazil. Controlling inflation involved official and private austerity and Brazilian politicians didn't want to hear the word "austerity" mentioned. They were big spenders. They had a vested interest in inflation.

In the early days of the Alliance for Progress our government gave preferential support to countries that exhibited the best national programs. But preparing programs, as we have seen, is comparatively simple. It is carrying them out that is difficult. Carrying out a program requires the cooperation of many persons and groups. The best prepared program can be overturned by a succeeding administration. What is most needed in Latin America is not programs but good faith, continuity, maturity in short.

What the United States government has a right to expect of aid recipients in Latin America is a generous degree of bipartisanship with reference to economic development. Without bipartisanship in the United States and in the European countries receiving our aid, the Marshall Plan would have had no chance of succeeding. Nor will Latin American countries be able to take reasonable advantage of foreign aid, public or private, unless they demonstrate a comparable degree of bipartisanship.

The United States government, as well as private capital in the United States and other countries, could do no less than give extraordinary support to a country whose leading political groups were demonstrating a maturity that, in general, has been lacking in Latin America and that, if present, would insure progress. In the absence of such evidence of maturity the United States government would do well to move slowly and cautiously in the aid field. Deliberateness, no matter what pejorative term our ideologists and activists may use to describe it, is much more likely to encourage maturity and progress than the emotional haste, even demagogy, with which our government launched the Alliance for Progress.

It will not be a simple task for Latin Americans in political life to improve their performance. It is easier for them to disagree with each other than to agree. From the short-term viewpoint it is frequently more profitable to tear down than to help build. Demagogy has been a reliable device for winning elections, and it will not be given up easily. However, like my Latin American friends, I see no other way. Continuous economic improvement will come to Latin America together with political improvement, if it comes at all. The other elements for progress exist. They include trade, aid, the good will of the more developed countries. But not all these will be available in full measure indefinitely. An aid program that does not produce results will not receive American support forever.

Nationalism and provincialism are devices that Latin Americans have used to protect themselves from their own inadequacies or fancied inadequacies. But they no longer protect, if indeed they ever did. Rather they tend to prolong and add to inadequacy.

Nationalism and provincialism, and the demagogy they nourish, will not disappear overnight or during our lifetime. But if deterioration is to be avoided, they must be combated more energetically than they have been in the past. And those who must take the lead in combating them are the same political leaders who up to now have indulged in them and also, of course, the new leaders who are emerging, many of whom are intimately familiar with the wider world of which Latin America is a part and to which it must do its share of adjusting if it is to advance.

A Selected Bibliography

Anderson, Charles W. *Politics and Economic Change in Latin America: The Governing of Restless Nations.* Princeton, Van Nostrand, 1967.

Beaulac, Willard L. *Career Ambassador.* New York, Macmillan, 1951.

———. *Career Diplomat.* New York, Macmillan, 1964.

Berle, Adolf A. *Latin America, Diplomacy and Reality.* New York, Harper & Row, 1962.

Black, Eugene R. *The Diplomacy of Economic Development.* Cambridge, Harvard University, 1960.

Brandenburg, Frank. *The Development of Latin American Private Enterprise.* Washington, D. C., National Planning Assn., 1964.

de Oliveira Campos, Roberto. *Reflections on Latin American Development.* Austin, University of Texas, 1967.

Dreier, John, ed. *The Alliance for Progress: Problems and Prospects.* Baltimore, Johns Hopkins, 1962.

Eisenhower, Dwight D. *Waging Peace.* Garden City, Doubleday, 1965.

Elliott, William Y. *Education and Training in the Developing Countries: The Role of U.S. Foreign Aid.* New York, Praeger, 1966.

Feis, Herbert. *Foreign Aid and Foreign Policy.* New York, St. Martins, 1964.

Gordon, Lincoln. *A New Deal for Latin America: The Alliance for Progress.* Cambridge, Harvard University, 1963.

Hirschman, Albert O. *Journeys toward Progress: Studies in Economic Policy-Making in Latin America.* New York, Twentieth Century Fund, 1963.

Kindleberger, Charles P. *American Business Abroad: Six Lectures on Direct Investment.* New Haven, Yale University, 1969.

Lieuwen, Edwin. *Arms and Politics in Latin America,* rev. ed. New York, Praeger, 1967.

Marshall, Charles Burton. *The Exercise of Sovereignty.* Baltimore, Johns Hopkins, 1965.

———. *The Limits of Foreign Policy,* enl. ed. Baltimore, Johns Hopkins, 1968.

Montgomery, John D. *Foreign Aid in International Politics.* Englewood Cliffs, Prentice-Hall, 1967.

Myint, Hia. *The Economics of the Developing Countries.* New York, Praeger, 1964.

Nixon, Richard M. *Six Crises.* New York, Pyramid, 1962.

Pincus, John. *Trade, Aid and Development: The Rich and Poor Nations.* New York, McGraw-Hill, 1967.

Powelson, John P. *Latin America: Today's Economic and Social Revolution.* New York, McGraw-Hill, 1964.

Taylor, D. *Development Means People.* New York, Pergamon, 1964.

Waterston, Albert. *Development Planning: Lessons of Experience.* Baltimore, Johns Hopkins, 1965.

Wiggins, J. S., and Helmut Schoeck, eds. *Foreign Aid Reexamined—A Critical Appraisal.* Washington, D. C., Public Affairs Press, 1958.

Index

DATE DUE
FEB 22 1971
MAR 29 1971
MAY 17 1971
APR 16 1973
JUN 14 1971
MAY 10 1976
MAR 2 9 2002
OCT 7 1982
APR 2 5 1997
DEC 0 6 1997
MAR 3 0 1999